To Mary,

I am

at your service.

Ann Marie Gorczyca

Praise for *At Your Service*

Once you pick this book up you won't want to put it down. Ann Marie Gorczyca is a leading authority in Dental Practice Owner Education, and is a world-renowned successful author in that field. In this, her latest book, Ann Marie teaches you all the little intricacies that you need to know to build a world-class customer focused dental practice. If you aspire to build the best Dental Office ever, then you need to read this book and you need everyone in your organization to read this book. This book is a true "How To" book written by someone who walks the walk in every sense of the word. Every dentist needs to read this book.

-Dr. David Moffet BDS FPFA CSP
The #1 Authority on World Class Dental Customer Service and Author
of the Amazon #1 Bestseller *How to Build the Dental Practice of Your Dreams [Without Killing Yourself!] In Less Than 60 Days*

At Your Service is a reminder that customer/patient service is more than just taking care of teeth. It's about building a successful practice with a reputation for delivering an amazing patient experience. This is a book that every dentist should read before they graduate dental school. Don't just be a good dentist. Be a successful dentist. This book will help take your practice from good to ...*amazing!*

-Shep Hyken, customer service expert and *New York Times*
Best Selling Author of *The Amazement Revolution*

At Your Service shares customer service tips important not only for dentistry, but for all industries. Customer experience cultures are rare, and yet the financial impact of a focus on customers is massive. A five percent increase in customer retention can boost profits as much as eighty-five percent. Creating a customer focused culture will help make your dental practice not only more profitable, but memorable, enjoyable, and even exceptional. This book will help you create an exceptional service experience.

-Dave Kerpen, Likeable CEO,
NY Times Best Selling Author & Keynote Speaker

Dr. Ann Marie Gorczyca's latest book, *At You Service* is a must-read for any business that wants to be known for excellence in service to its patients/customers. The beauty of this book is that it is loaded with effective, easy to implement ideas that will wow your patients and turn them into an avid voluntary sales force! Dr. Gorczyca has shared the ideas, beliefs, and convictions that have been the foundation of her outstanding success; and her willingness to share them with others is a demonstration of her commitment to her profession and to patients everywhere.

-Joan Garbo, Consultant, Trainer, Speaker

At Your Service is a 'five-star' comprehensive look at what dental practices can do to achieve excellence in customer service. Dr. Ann Marie Gorczyca has created an insightful, example-filled, pragmatic resource to improve the quality and consistency of care by dentists and dental teams for their customers—their patients. This is a timely resource for today's dental practice where it's not enough to just offer 'good treatment.' In the 21st century, it is more important than ever to treat each patient with outstanding customer service. This book offers many superb pearls which will enhance the quality of your patient experience. Every member of your customer service team will find *At Your Service* to be an excellent reference for dental practice success.

-S. Jay Bowman, DMD, MSD, Orthodontist, Kalamazoo Orthodontics

Dr. Ann Marie Gorczyca's book *At Your Service* is an inspiration to those who serve the customer in all service organizations. The principles and ideas in this book will add value to your service leadership growth and elevate your service excellence to the next level. Service contributions from the hospitality perspective are here to energize service leaders everywhere.

-Tal Shnall, Customer Service Trainer, Speaker

When it comes to five-star customer service, everything matters. Dr. Ann Marie Gorczyca's new book *At Your Service* draws together many critical service areas to lift your practice high above the average. This book emphasizes the soft side of customer engagement done well. I highly recommend this book because five-star service is what we aim to deliver and all yearn to receive.

-Bill Williams, DMD, MAGD, SolsticeDentalAdvisors.com
Author of *Marketing the Million Dollar Practice*

When I visit a new client, one of the first things I notice is the bookshelf in their office. I love to peruse the titles and get a feel for what fills their minds. Dr. Ann Marie Gorczyca's third book, *At Your Service,* is a resource that I'd be thrilled to see on the reading list of every practice. Ann Marie has done an exceptional job of overlaying the experience she delivers consistently in her dental practice with what she has learned from customer service leaders outside of dentistry. A focus on the small touches can transform a 'visit' into an 'experience' and she presents a step-by-step approach in a simple-to-use guide. Brava Doc! I'm looking forward to referring your book to some of my Crews!

-T. Andre Shirdan, Coach, Motivational Speaker,
and Creator of The Crew Process

At Your Service

Five-Star Customer Care for a Successful Dental Practice

DR. ANN MARIE GORCZYCA

Copyright © 2017 by Dr. Ann Marie Gorczyca. All rights reserved.

No part of this publication may be reproduced, stored in a retrieval system, or transmitted in any form or by any means, electronic, mechanical, photocopying, recording, scanning, or otherwise, without the prior written permission of the authors.

Limit of Liability/Disclaimer of Warranty: While the publisher and authors have used their best efforts in preparing this book, they make no representations or warranties with respect to the accuracy or completeness of the contents of this book and specifically disclaim any implied warranties of merchantability or fitness for a particular purpose. No warranty may be created or extended by sales representatives or written sales materials. The advice and strategies contained herein may not be suitable for your situation. You should consult with a professional when appropriate. Neither the publisher nor the authors shall be liable for any loss of profit or any other commercial damages, including but not limited to special, incidental, consequential, personal, or other damages.

At Your Service
Five-Star Customer Care for a Successful Dental Practice
By Ann Marie Gorczyca

1. MED 016090 Medical: Dentistry - Practice Management
2. MED 016000 Medical: Dentistry - General
3. BUS 043000 Business & Economics: Marketing - General

ISBN-13: 978-1-935953-83-8

Interior design by JETLAUNCH

Printed in the United States of America

Authority Publishing
11230 Gold Express Dr. #310-413
Gold River, CA 95670
800-877-1097
www.AuthorityPublishing.com

To my grandmother, Babcie,
    immigrant, wife, mother,
    seamstress, farmer, cook,
    director of the family farm stand,
    and delighter of customers.

Thank you
    for everything you taught me.

CONTENTS

Foreword ix
Introduction xiii
How to Use This Book xvii

PART I: CULTURE 1

Chapter 1:   Leadership 5
Chapter 2:   Trust 21
Chapter 3:   Ownership 31
Chapter 4:   Communication 43
Chapter 5:   Alignment 61
Chapter 6:   Results 69
Chapter 7:   Excellence 81

PART II: CARE 87

Chapter 8:   Friendliness 89
Chapter 9:   Attitude 99
Chapter 10: Engagement 107
Chapter 11: Smile 119
Chapter 12: Appearance 127
Chapter 13: Impression 131

PART III: CLIMATE 137

Chapter 14: Empowerment 139
Chapter 15: Preparedness 151
Chapter 16: Assistance 165
Chapter 17: Fulfillment 171
Chapter 18: Creativity 179
Chapter 19: Preservation 187
Chapter 20: Five-Star Customer Service 201

Conclusion 209
Appendix 1: Calendar Template 211
Appendix 2: Sample Calendar 212
Acknowledgements 213
About the Author 217
Bibliography 219

FOREWORD

"*The customer is always right!*" This is one sentence that anyone who has worked in a service industry has heard at least a million times. Those of us who work directly with customers most likely recite this mantra in our sleep with the number of times it's been ingrained through countless training meetings, seminars, and workshops. Yet, this universally accepted adage couldn't be further from the truth. Customers are NOT always right. In fact, customers are wrong... a lot. Customers break things, misunderstand policies, and almost never actually read instructions. However, regardless what a customer has done or not done, one fact remains a fundamental truth to organizations who depend on customers: while the customer is NOT always right, they are ALWAYS the customer. Serving customers is an intensely personal human interaction, and these interactions are occurring all of the time. In some way, shape, or form, every individual in an organization contributes to a customer's overall experience.

Today we are in the midst of a revolution of historic proportions. Experts have termed this dramatic shift in the balance of power as the beginning of the "Age of the Customer." While advancements in technology and access to information have given us new gadgets, features, products, and expanded opportunities for services not available to previous generations, present customers continue to grow restless. The simmering impatience and frustration isn't because of the costs of goods and services. Despite the level of advancement in technologies, they remain remarkably affordable. It isn't due to lack of features or functionality. On the contrary, products today seem to stretch most users' ability to take advantage of all possible applications. The growing sense of resentment

FOREWORD

and frustration from customers can be pinpointed to how many feel they are treated by the organizations meant to serve them and the lack of foresight into their actual wants and needs. Tired of mediocrity, customers today no longer just accept average as "that's just how business is done." With just a few keystrokes, a 140-character tweet, or a couple of sentences on a review site, the reputation of a business and its future opportunities for success hang in the balance.

The gap between the perception of services delivered and customers' satisfaction with those services continues to widen. This gulf between a customer and a service provider is a critical strategic variance that must be bridged if an organization wishes to retain its customers long-term and continue to grow in attracting new ones. A Bain & Company Service Delivery report showed that an astonishing 80% of businesses believed they delivered a superior customer service experience, while only 8% of their customers agreed that those same companies delivered a superior service experience. What's worse, when Bain surveyed the management team in those organizations, 95% of them believed that they were customer focused. The power of social networks has increased the impact of customer reviews today. In today's digital age, what your customers think and feel is processed at the speed of light and instantly distributed throughout the world for almost anyone to see. Word of mouth carries a big, heavy stick when it comes to the reputation of your business products and services. Half of customers today, in a study done by Satmetrix, cited recommendations from personal connections as a most trustworthy source of information. Facebook, Twitter, Yelp, and other social media and review sites help to amplify the voice of the customer. The Internet and its ability to expand our social connections has given incredible power to the voice of the customer. A single bad customer service experience posted online can spiral out of control, tarnishing the image of an organization that has taken years to build. The management expert Peter Drucker famously explained that the purpose of a business is to create and keep a customer. Fulfilling and sustaining that purpose long-term requires tight alignment between our actions as service providers and the needs and wants of the customer.

From a young age, Dr. Ann Marie Gorczyca has learned how to emotionally connect with customers while working on her family's fruit and vegetable stand. Those simple, yet powerful lessons learned have been instrumental in developing a successful orthodontics practice beloved by its clients. In her playbook for personal care service providers, Dr. Gorczyca masterfully outlines how dentists, dental teams, and other personal care professionals can make exceptional positive impact in the treatment of their patients. The practical tactical insight provided in *At Your Service* is applicable, now more than ever, to anyone who works directly with customers, regardless of industry. From how to establish a base of trust and communication between your team members, to how to approach daily interactions with customers so that you always make everyone feel special, Dr. Gorczyca will guide you through the process of establishing a winning service-focused organization. As we continue to see the evolution in customer-focused service and customer experience as a strategic differentiator, *At Your Service* should be a required instruction manual for anyone working in a service industry. Dr. Gorczyca has mastered the art of experience while building a practice with a growing base of raving fans. She encourages all of us to change our mentality in our approach from serving "customers" to serving family and friends, because the individuals you serve *are* family and friends to someone, and their overall experience will greatly impact not only their relationship with your organization but also their opinion of your organization. To remain relevant in business today, we must be more focused on developing relationships than on performing transactions.

As a passionate practitioner of customer care excellence, Dr. Gorczyca's approach helps us to develop the necessary framework for creating teams of service-focused, customer-centered specialists. With her Harvard School of Dental Medicine education and modern approach to customer experience, Dr. Gorczyca's *At Your Service* serves as a guide through the journey of developing a culture of service and walks through the tactical considerations to properly prepare your team to act. As you follow her methods to establish a climate where continual service improvement can take place, you will see a transformation in the relationship between you and your clients. Dr. Gorczyca leads her team through example, and the results are indisputable. The Gorczyca team foundation consists of three core principles: clinical excellence, outstanding service, and great patient experience. The culture they've developed unites them in principle and purpose. The love of service and the attention to care isn't just a motto, it's something that permeates every aspect of the Gorczyca Orthodontics experience. It's not every day that you'll hear someone admit they're excited to see their dentist, but Dr. Gorczyca, her bright smile, her fla-

FOREWORD

vored dental gloves, and her team deliver on a new level of enthusiasm, dedication, and customer delight. When you're fortunate to have this team care for you, you're truly counting down the hours until your next appointment.

-Flavio Marins is COO of DigiCert, Inc. and the author of *Win the Customer: 70 Simple Rules for Sensational Service (2016)*

INTRODUCTION

Either write something worth reading or
do something worth writing.
-Benjamin Franklin

Smiles change lives. It's the reason we love our jobs, love our patients, and are eager to go to work in the morning. Our patients and their families and friends are our customers. This customer will be influenced by the service we give. We want that service experience to be five-star.

I've seen over and over again the positive impact that dentistry has on a person's life. From the child who tried to commit suicide because the kids at school called him "Bucky Beaver" before being saved by mandibular distraction osteogenesis, to the forty-year-old woman who has a smile makeover and found true love for the first time, our work in dentistry allows our patients to smile from ear to ear. Improving your patient's smile gives them new confidence and happiness. Dentistry changes our patients' lives forever.

Outstanding customer service is a primary goal of every dental office. Great service is created and nurtured by culture. It is created by the leadership of the doctor producing trust, ownership, communication, and alignment of the team. Once a service culture is in place, office results will be excellent. When culture, care, and climate are excellent, it's a five-star experience not only for the patients, but also for the doctor and team.

To achieve great customer service in your dental office, start by making the patient your highest priority. Everything we do, and our reason for being at work in dentistry, is for the patient. No matter how you are feeling, or whatever the distractions that may be present in your personal or

INTRODUCTION

professional life, once the patient arrives, *that* is priority one. Here lies the essence of outstanding customer service: focused, individualized attention given to the patient.

I first learned about customer service as a child working on my family's farm stand. The stand's owner, my Polish immigrant grandmother, arrived in the United States alone at age sixteen to make a new life for herself. When I was six, my grandmother gave me a job selling the fruits and vegetables. She valued and recognized customer service. She told me to look cute, smile, and make the customers happy. Make them feel special. Do something a little extra just for them. Say to them, "Mrs. Ashley, please allow me to give you this delicious cucumber especially for you today." And so my education in customer service began.

Owning a business can be fun. It allows us to make people happy. To do so effectively, one must learn to focus on the customer and leave personal cares and troubles behind. When you love people, they will love you in return. When you are happy, you will make other people happy.

Making people happy need not be hard. Give them a smile. Tell them you are happy to see them. Give them a gift. Tell them it is your pleasure to serve them. Thank them for their visit, and that you will look forward to seeing them, as well as their friends and family in the future.

Sometimes, the stress of an unfilled schedule or other pressure may divert attention from such "small" talk. Instead of focusing on the relationship with happy patients present in the office, the dentist or team member may focus precious mental energy on potential patients not present. On a busy day in the dental office, team members may feel rushed by a tight schedule or an unexpected emergency appointment. The dental team may not deliver the level of customer service which the dentist desires. He or she is focused on an uninspired team member rather than the customer—the valuable dental patient. In both these ways, customer service declines.

Without our customers, our satisfied patients, we would be out of business. Customer service may be something dentists do not wish to emphasize, but they must. For everyone running a successful dental practice, customer service is a critical element of the business management mix.

As an orthodontic specialist for over twenty-seven years, I've heard some patients talk about their dentist with love, while others say they would never return to a dental office again. Yet there are dental patients who will drive hours or hundreds of miles for outstanding customer service from their favorite dental professional.

FIVE STAR PATIENT CARE

What uniqueness is it that makes a five-star customer service dental office? These teams deliver at every touchpoint of the patient's total office experience. Their actions attend to every aspect of the patient's comfort and feeling of fulfillment in the dental office. The patient feels that they are getting high value for their money not only in terms of their dental care, but also with respect to their overall patient experience.

Outstanding customer service teams know that every dental patient is unique. Some require minimal attention and some are high maintenance. Everyone in the office needs to know each patient personally, including their expectations, desires, and goals of treatment in order to give them the highest level of personalized customer care.

Customer service can easily be ignored, until someone describes your office's poor patient experience on Yelp and gives you a one-star review. When this happens, consider it a gift. There is a solution to every customer service complaint. Now you have the opportunity to improve. Thank the patient for calling the issue to your attention. Once the problem is resolved, you have the opportunity to create an adoring fan. By eliminating those complaints that we are fortunate to know about, we can all strive to never have a patient complaint in the first place.

We can all get five-star reviews. Outstanding customer service just takes time and attention. Start by remembering "It's Showtime!" and everyone in the office needs to be in on the act. Together, the ensemble can create a memorable service culture.

The goal is to create outstanding customer service *systems* so that the dentist can then focus on rendering excellent dental patient care. The last thing that any patient should ever experience in the dental office is rudeness, apathy, or lack of empathy. Outstanding dental team customer service leaders will work well together, ultimately delighting patients while producing dental practice success. To do this, dentists need to get customer service right the first time.

To some dental professionals, "soft skills" come naturally. For others, customer service tips need to be reviewed for best practices, in order to acquire emotional intelligence and other acumen. To those who need to

INTRODUCTION

work on their customer service skills, the information in this book will be helpful.

When I was a student at the Harvard School of Dental Medicine, I had the opportunity to study at Harvard School of Public Health in the Department of Health Management and Policy. There, I attended management lectures and started to understand the importance and broad-reaching effects of customer service within the broader healthcare service industry, including dentistry.

It was not until I stayed at my first five-star hotel that I truly understood customer delight and the business benefits of outstanding customer service. The hotel hospitality business truly leads the way in this regard.

When I started teaching at The University of the Pacific, Arthur A. Dugoni School of Dentistry, we added a customer service course to the business management curriculum. We reviewed the impact of such terms as "My pleasure" versus "No problem." Aiming to remain relevant and memorable, we gave a Customer Service Award to the most service-oriented resident. We also give an annual Customer Service Award at Gorczyca Orthodontics. This is the highest award achievable in the dental office. The successful team member gets a cash award and a special pin. The recipient's name is listed in our Team Handbook.

Five-star customer service is something each of us can deliver. Outstanding customer service is the end that we wish to achieve, day after day, year after year. This book will describe the *means* to this *end*.

In the past, dental offices often used questionnaires to obtain patient service metrics. In the age of social media, customer online reviews now take away this administrative task. Social media sites, such as Yelp, Facebook, and Google, give dentists immediate responses regarding their service each day. Once feedback is acquired, education, organization, and implementation of customer service systems can be undertaken. This requires time, attention, and a team devoted to working together to produce immediate service results.

Dentistry is, after all, a *service* industry. It is a business, but we should never lose sight of the fact that we are providing Service. The definition of a "profession" is that we put others above ourselves. First, last, and always, we are here to serve our patients, who also happen to be customers. That is why outstanding customer service is so central to a successful practice. Now, let's get started.

HOW TO USE THIS BOOK

*The purpose of business
is to create and keep a customer.*
-Peter Drucker

Customer service is a combination of small actions put together to make the patient feel great about their experience. Delivery of outstanding customer service requires prompt and polite actions delivered by you and your team. The final step is the development, organization, and implementation of a customer service plan. All of these, together, produce the customer service experience.

Customer service can be divided into three main categories:

I. Culture: How your team delivers outstanding customer service.
II. Care: How your care feels to the patient and their family.
III. Climate: Systems and management of five-star customer service.

This book outlines strategies to create an outstanding culture, care, and climate, producing a remarkable customer service experience. To explain these activities, I have written descriptions of things to consider when delivering outstanding customer service in the dental office.

All dentists work in a business within the healthcare service industry. We provide many dental products and services. How well we deliver this service in the eyes, hearts, and minds of the customer will determine our success.

HOW TO USE THIS BOOK

We need a kind, caring, and professional team to deliver our product: dental health. Each team member is a customer service leader. Our customer experience will therefore only be as good as our weakest link on our customer service chain.

How well you organize, manage, implement, and measure your customer experience is critical to your success. Spending time on customer service education, organization, and implementation will benefit your practice. Customer service is a key element of the dental business management mix.

As you read through the customer service topics, tips, and stories in this book, you will be able to construct your own customer service calendar (Appendix). Plan action items from each of the book's three parts: Culture, Care, and Climate. Write the projects initiated on the calendar. See programs through to completion. Once you have launched your customer service plan, keep track of your compliments and five-star reviews. Eliminate complaints by focusing on areas of needed improvement. Keep track of your results in a small notebook to be reviewed at your daily, weekly, or monthly team meetings.

Ask patients "How are we doing?" and "How was your visit today?" This is the best customer service feedback you will ever get. Once you have reviewed and analyzed your results, take action. Eliminate service troubles and replace them with delights. Produce an outstanding patient experience through the climate, care, and culture of your dental office.

Part I

CULTURE

*When we're confronted by
spectacular success or failure,
everyone from the CEO to the janitor
points in the same direction:
the culture.*
                        -Margaret Heffernan

It is independent of price and product. It is not a function of high salaries or educational degrees. It's not a fancy imaging machine, dental restoration, or a procedure. Delivering winning customer service is an individual mission of each dental leader and a product of office culture. It's something special that cannot be duplicated. Your culture is something that only you and your dental team can create.

Your culture distinguishes you from all other dental offices in the world. It's how you treat human beings, your dental patients, one at a time, with attention, action, and tender loving care.

In order to create, develop, and protect your customer-centric culture, it's important for the leader and everyone on the team to clearly understand that your very existence as a dental office depends on your customers: the patients. The customer pays your salary. Once everyone understands and accepts this fact, it will be much easier to embed the customer experience as the central point of your office culture.

Your office culture is your brand. Culture is not optional. Culture is not negotiable. It is there for total engagement by everyone on your team and especially the leader. The production and maintenance of your customer service culture is the most important job requirement of everyone in the business of dentistry. We are employed to serve the patient. Your customer service is the life blood of your dental business.

At Gorczyca Orthodontics, we have three core values: clinical excellence, outstanding customer service, and a great patient experience. Culture and core values are maintained as part of the job requirements. These standards are clearly written in the policy and procedure manual, the Team Handbook. Every team member can recite the three core values by heart. The customer service standards outlined within your Team Handbook cannot and should not be lowered.

A key to maintenance of an outstanding culture is to eliminate poor performers while developing all performers to the level of excellent. This action is the responsibility of leadership. Time and effort must be devoted to training and development of everyone onboard.

Building an office culture focused on customer service starts on day one for the new hire. The first day of employment is the most important day for a new "service leader." It sets the tone of what either becomes a dental career veteran or a transient employee. Customer service orientation is described in your Team Handbook. Dress code is specified. Smiling is a requirement. From the outset, team members are expected to work together for the best interest of the patient and the success of the dental office.

Dental leaders must communicate customer service goals on a daily basis to continuously foster engagement. Review past successes and other positive patient experiences regularly. Read customer service five-star reviews on Yelp and other review sites with your team. Keep five-star service top of mind. More importantly, read and respond to anything less than five stars within the business day. Improve areas less than five stars immediately.

Thank team members for customer service jobs well done. Give recognition for outstanding customer service to help your team to achieve even more five-star reviews. An annual customer service award can be one special way the entire team can focus on rewarding customer excellence. Have team members vote for who they feel deserves the Customer Service Award. Every team member's voice is heard and everyone's opinion counts. Make the annual Customer Service Award the highest recognition in your office. Place each winner's name in your Team Handbook or on a special plaque.

What gets rewarded gets repeated. Ask your team, "What can we continue to do to make us even better in the eyes, hearts, and minds of our patients?" Keep track of the patient responses. Is your dental office culture producing happiness, joy, and excitement in engaged and referring patients? Or, is it producing something else? For the best customer service results, embed learning and improvement of the customer experience into your dental office culture.

Chapter 1

LEADERSHIP

People who add value to others do so intentionally.
To add value, leaders must give of themselves,
and that rarely occurs by accident.
                                      -John C. Maxwell

I wish there were a course in dental school called "Leadership." It would teach dentists that leadership requires courage, communication, candor, and action. Leadership requires persistence, and lots of it. As you lead, you will constantly be on the move, implementing change and solutions by what you learn, observe, and hear. You will be continuously making adjustments to produce the maximal success of your organization. Achieving this goal will necessarily include five-star customer service.

Truth is a sign of great leadership. Superficial congeniality gets you nowhere. A leader deals with realities, not just niceties. A leader doesn't wish things were better. A leader makes things better. A leader encounters life as it is, day by day, and is prepared to deal with whatever happens, expected or unexpected.

How many times have you been to a fine restaurant and during the meal the owner comes to your table to inquire about your dining experience? A service culture starts with the head and heart of the owner. This is the leader. Service starts at the top with service leadership.

The first person you will lead is yourself. Before you influence others, lead others, motivate others, or change others, you must first identify, state, and document that which you are trying to achieve. If we influence our team to serve, then we must first serve. We, after all, lead by example.

A leader will need to anticipate, adapt to, and foster change, successfully implementing solutions. Change is inevitable. Every day something will change in your dental office. Transformational leadership is the ability to influence the team to carry out changes needed to achieve the goals of your dental practice. Leadership leads change.

John Maxwell, in his book *The Five Levels of Leadership*, defines leadership by five levels:

1. Right
2. Respect
3. Relationships
4. Results
5. Recruitment

THE FIVE Rs OF LEADERSHIP

1. RIGHT

*Clarity is the beginning
of a good experience.*
-Skip Prichard

Whether it be a business leader like Jack Welch or a military leader like Napoleon Bonaparte, leaders stand alone and have a clear voice. Leaders have a position that only they can create. As a dentist who runs an office, you have taken the *risk* of business ownership, earning the *right* of leadership. But that is only the start of your leadership journey. One *responsibility* of your leadership is to get the best performance out of your people. Another aim is to make your dental office the most successful it can be. A third goal is to be inspirational to others, while creating an enjoyable culture for your patients, for your team, and for yourself.

A role of leadership is to ask, "Are team members actively engaged?"

Or, are they just punching the clock? Do they stay after the patient care day ends, or do they rush out the door? Are they team players? Do they ask each other if they can help, or do they run out like it is a "fire drill?" If an individual leaves as soon as possible, they are working only for the paycheck. You have not yet inspired them. You're not yet a transformational leader. You have only the "right" of leadership, the position.

Transformational leaders inspire teams to transcend their own self-interests. The highest form of transformational leadership is idealized influence. Here, office goals are clearly explained, set forth, implemented, managed, and reviewed in a charismatic manner. Everyone is on-board and excited to be part of the vision. Once this is accomplished, team members feel a personal stake in everything they do. They have made a 100 percent commitment.

2. RESPECT

> *Respect a man,*
> *and he will do all the more.*
> -John Wooden

If you want it as a leader, you've got to give it. Respect is a two-way street. Leadership is influence. To gain influence, the leader must enable a culture of mutual respect in the office. The simple act of paying positive attention to people on your customer service team has a great deal to do with how well they perform, their level of productivity, and the customer experience which they deliver.

A culture of customer service is a culture of respect. The respect you give each other will make your work fulfilling and valued. It will be evident to everyone that their work is important.

There are several ways that you can convey respect in the workplace. Give each person the opportunity to express their ideas. Tokens and kind words of appreciation are perhaps the most powerful ways. Welcome team suggestions and feedback. Value everyone's contributions and views. Acknowledge all contributions to the success of the dental office.

As the leader, it is imperative that you adhere to the goals and core values of the office, maintaining policy and procedures, as well as respectful and professional behavior. There will be different levels of respect with different team members. It will take time to earn the respect of a recently hired team member as the leader since you have not yet been fully acquainted and tested. Some new hires are less experienced and therefore not aware of the work and commitment of more veteran employees. During the transition of on-boarding, there will inevitably be adjustment and accommodations, but there may even be dissent from young, new team members.

Don't let the tail try to wag the dog. Hold true to your core values. Don't tolerate substandard behavior. The first time you do, you will be perceived as a weak leader, and your authority and respect will be diminished or lost forever. If you are not a strong leader, the strongest personality in your office will take control of your culture.

The leader must never compromise on their ethics. There will be challenges and dilemmas you will face. A patient may ask you to bill insurance in a certain way or debit their medical savings account on a certain date that you ethically (and legally) cannot do. Don't do it. Always do the right thing. Walk away from situations where the morals of your office would be compromised in any way.

Dentists are usually the "first-in last-out" employees in the office. Your work ethic should speak for itself. Lead by example. The dentist sets the example of work ethic and customer service they desire for the team. When you work hard and achieve excellence, your work is respected.

When you follow and enforce the rules, good guys win and bad guys go home. By sticking to the HR rules, you eliminate the possibility of making bad choices, especially when it comes to fairness. Leaders must respect office policies and treat everyone fairly.

3. RELATIONSHIPS

Leaders must be close enough to relate to others,
but far enough ahead to motivate them.
-John C. Maxwell

As you begin your journey of becoming a transformational leader, you will be converting your people from "having to serve" to "wanting to serve" to "loving to serve." You're growing and grooming your team to have a caring attitude. By spending time and attention on relationships, you are building a high-performance team of service leaders. The office's customer service ethos will need to be their shared values. They will need to believe in the mission. Your dental office will become a place where team members want to work and where they feel a sense of belonging.

It is essential to have a good working relationship with your team members. You cannot influence someone whom you antagonize or don't like, and vice versa. Hire individuals who give you a positive gut feeling, who resonate good vibes, and who, like you, are motivated by relationships with other team members and their patients. If you are not feeling this from a present team member, *it is time to act* in your role of leadership and make a change for the improvement of your dental office. This is the toughest aspect of leadership needed to build and preserve a positive office culture.

How do you influence your team to foster positive relationships? You are, after all, together in the quest to build a successful dental office. Each team member needs to understand that they are a stakeholder in the outcome of their own work. One way to build this ethic is through transparency. Be open with your practice numbers. Review metrics and key result indicators often. Make the goals known and embraced by all. Work on achieving your goals, together, as a team.

You will positively influence your team relationships by being totally involved and fully present. Walk around your office. Listen, and observe all that is taking place. Talk to each person, each day individually. Ask them how they are doing. Give one-on-one feedback. Ask your team members where they need help. Follow up on office projects. Give appreciation and praise. Reward jobs well done.

Meet regularly with your team of customer service leaders for monthly meetings and annual "Advances" (not "Retreats"). Prepare, moderate, and follow through with the action items discussed. Participate in team-continuing education. To jump start engagement, try this: present each of your customer service leaders with a book. The book is titled *Becoming the Most Customer-Centric Dental Office in the World*. They are the authors. The publishing date is in the future. Tell them, "This is the most important book you will ever read. It will be written by some of the highest authorities in patient satisfaction in dentistry: our team. Now open the book. The pages are blank because we will be writing the book together. We begin today."

Relationships equal results. Office relationships are within your control. Celebrate every success. Correct every failure. Now the same emphasis that is placed on clinical excellence and financial achievement is placed on customer service and patient experience. Brava and bravo!

4. RESULTS

> *Effective leadership is putting first things first.*
> *Effective management is discipline, carrying it out.*
> -Stephen R. Covey

The notable authority on leadership and transformational change, Dr. John Kotter, states that leadership must create a sense of urgency in order to guide a coalition to successful outcomes. By providing the tools that your team needs to realize patient-centric service, you will be well on the way to reaching desired and durable practice results.

You can't send people where they've never been. Your commitment to customer service education helps you and your team to produce the five-star service results you desire. Education will create momentum in the attention, engagement, implementation, and production of outstanding customer service results. Time devoted to patient-centric training will also help you attract and retain team members with a passion for service.

People do what they see and hear. In order to produce customer service results, you need to provide the materials that your team needs to get started. This includes materials for training and re-training. One exceptional book is *180 Ways to Walk the Customer Service Talk* by Eric Harvey. One year, my office used this small book as the foundation of an all-day team "Advance" on customer service. Both the book and the off-site team building Advance were excellent resources for preparing our team to become brand ambassadors in the delivery of an exceptional patient care experience.

At Walt Disney World, leaders in customer service have a tradition called "good show/bad show." Here, performance tips are given to improve quality of service. You can do the same in your dental office at your monthly team meetings.

Customer service training is a continuous process which can be perfected. Reading books, focusing on service at team meetings, reviewing feedback from patient surveys, and scheduling enabling attendance at continuing education courses, empower your office leaders with more knowledge and power to serve. The most effective leaders transform knowledge and training sessions into visible action. A leader thereby *encourages* every member of the team to produce customer service *results*.

5. RECRUITMENT

> *The first ten people will determine*
> *whether the company succeeds or not.*
> *Each is 10 percent of the company.*
> *So why wouldn't you take as much time*
> *as necessary to find all the A players?*
> *A small company depends on great people*
> *much more than a big company does.*
> -Steve Jobs

Often the best way to avoid leadership problems is to recruit people with "the right stuff." In dentistry, just as with any team, you need to *recruit* the best players on the market. Consider them your Smile Team. Leadership begins with assembling a team and developing their skills, while keeping them engaged, enthusiastic, and happy along the way. You will be a better coach with better players. The more capable and talented your team players, the better are your odds at winning. If you don't know what you're looking for, then you won't know it when you see it. It's important that the leader know what positions need to be filled, and what type of person will have the requisite qualities.

If delivering great customer service is your goal, start with a smile when considering potential hires. You can't make people smile. You need to find and employ happy individuals, who love people, and want to help people. You may ask, "How do you enjoy helping people?" as an interview question.

By completing rigorous dental education, you have earned *respect*, which you mirror to those around you. By *risking* the *responsibility of small business*, you have earned the *right* to be boss. But to be a leader, you must focus on *relationships* that are the foundation for lasting *results*. And it all begins with *recruitment*. Follow the adage: "hire slowly, fire quickly." Let your office culture of customer service be the beacon light that attracts and retains high quality, long-term, satisfied, and successful team members.

Your Core Values

> *When your values are clear to you,*
> *making decisions becomes easier.*
> -Roy E. Disney

To work well together, team members will need to know and respect the Core Values of the practice. If you understand your Core Values, you live your Core Values. At Gorczyca Orthodontics, our customer service leaders recite our three Core Values each year at our annual Advance and during their personal annual review. We recite our Core Values when people ask us, "Tell me about Gorczyca Orthodontics."

> *Our Core Values:*
> *Clinical excellence*
> *Outstanding customer service*
> *A great patient experience*

Your Core Values may also include your commitment to family. Let each team member have a picture of their family at their work station, and place a picture of the doctor's family in the exam room. This will serve as a constant source of happiness throughout the day and give your patients a human connection to the team member serving them.

Your Mission

> *All your customers are*
> *partners in your mission.*
> -Shep Hyken

Years ago, we created a Mission Statement. It was a description of what we aimed to achieve at Gorczyca Orthodontics. We met as a team and listed thoughts, feelings, and terms of what we wanted to achieve. Our descriptive Mission Statement went like this:

Our Mission:
To treat each patient, one at a time, with tender loving care.
To provide the finest orthodontic result
in a beautiful office with a warm, relaxed,
and professional environment.
To create a fun experience which instills well-being,
and fulfills even the unexpressed wishes and needs of our patients.
-Gorczyca Orthodontics

A Mission Statement is a call to action. It describes what you plan to do. It is a constant reminder of what you aim to achieve and deliver. The problem with our original Mission Statement was that it was too long. No one could remember it! So we sought to shorten it to look like those of Fortune 500 companies. These are short and effective. Let's look at some of those famous Mission Statements.

Provide the best customer service possible.
-Zappos

You're in good hands.
-Allstate

We try harder.
-Avis

Think different.
-Apple

Thrive.
-Kaiser-Permanente

Management guru Peter Drucker stated, "A mission statement should fit on the back of a T-shirt." I agree! Our actionable mission now reads:

Caring professionals serving valued patients.
-Gorczyca Orthodontics

LEADERSHIP

You will see our Mission Statement when you enter our office. It is behind our welcome concierge receptionist on our team "Wall of Fame." Each team member has a portrait on the wall with her name and job title. The doctor's picture also appears. This is our visual display of committed service. It exists to remind us and to promote customer engagement. We want our patients to know us by name. Our photos verify our commitment to our core mission.

Post your short Mission Statement. Memorize it. Remember it, live it, and deliver it. Let it guide you in your daily work.

Your Tag Line

Your smile is our inspiration.
-Gorczyca Orthodontics

It's the patient's smile which motivates us. The patient is why we exist as an orthodontic office and come to work each day. It's why we became dentists and entered the dental profession. Your Tag Line can be featured on your website and other promotional materials. Fashion your Tag Line to reflect what is uniquely your own within any given dental specialty.

Your Vision

We change lives by creating beautiful smiles.
-Gorczyca Orthodontics

Your vision is bigger than you. It is your calling. With your vision comes great responsibility to serve the patient well. It lets you know that you are doing important work. Team members should be able to read the vision, internalize it, live it, and let it encourage them to do excellent work and deliver outstanding customer service.

I was once having a mammogram done at UCSF medical center. I complimented the technician on her excellence of placing the imaging machine in difficult positions with speed and accuracy. She immediately replied, "We save lives." This was her vision for her work. She saw the big picture and realized the importance of her task. She had a purpose bigger than herself. She lived her vision.

Recently I bought a new car at Hansel Auto Group in Petaluma, California, and the service was impeccable. When the general manager came over to inquire how my experience had been that day, I could not hold back my praise and compliments. The manager responded that his company works hard on service values. He handed me a card, which all of his service leaders carried with them in their pocket as a constant reminder. As he would walk around the dealership, if he saw a service value being violated, the card would come out of his pocket and be hit three times on the desk or table as a reminder for the service leader to refocus on the service values. Here is the service card and what it read.

The front of the values card:

CARING DRIVES US
Hansel Auto Group
Customers
Co-workers
Community

The back of the values card:

OUR CORE VALUES
Trust-Respect-Integrity
Collaboration
Community
Innovation
Excellence

All I could say was WOW! The manager stated that it had taken his company over one year to come up with the tagline, mission, and core values of the company. They worked by, managed by, served by, studied, and lived by these values.

Take time to put together your own leadership values card. This can serve as the first chapter in your office customer service play book.

LEADERSHIP

Your Why

At well-led companies, people talk about the strength of the values.
At poorly led companies, people talk about the pay and benefits.
-Simon Sinek

Why do you do what you do? If you show up just for a paycheck, your work and service will be compromised and uninspired. When your personal purpose in life is to serve your patients, you will be inspired to provide the best customer service. You will be confident in your ability to provide great customer care.

It may surprise you that Walt Disney World and the Ritz-Carlton pay their workers the same as others in the industry. Customer service is not dependent on high rates of pay. Customer service is dependent on an attitude of service and belief in the service mission.

Outstanding customer service companies, such as the Ritz-Carlton, spend considerable time devoted to orientation and training. This is vital for customer care standards to be maintained. Twenty percent of the Ritz-Carlton's employees are dismissed within the first ninety days for unacceptable attendance. It may be the same for you in your dental office. The number one reason for dismissal at the Ritz-Carlton is poor attendance.

Take the time to give rigorous customer service education during your initial ninety-day orientation of new team members. Review language, dress code, teamwork, and immediate service recovery. It's not that well-led companies never hire people who end up being focused on pay and benefits. It's just that well-led companies keep employees focused on the customer.

Your Team

We ask ourselves what we wanted this company to stand for.
We didn't want to just sell shoes.
I wasn't even into shoes—
but I was passionate about customer service.
-Tony Hsieh

Hailed to be one of the greatest customer service businesses on earth, Zappos dedicates four weeks to training every employee before sending them off to answer calls. We often don't have the woman-power to make such an isolated dedication in dentistry, but we can make the commitment to training. The front desk is where the magic happens. At Zappos, rather than being focused on the number of calls received, they focus on developing a personal, emotional connection and building a relationship with the customer. This is the customer service training perspective and focus of America's top customer service company.

Founder of Zappos, Tony Hsieh, states that he views his role as setting up an environment where the personalities, creativity, and individuality of employees can come out and shine. This is similar to Google's focus on twenty percent of employee time being dedicated to what they are most passionate about. We can do the same in our dental office.

Unleashing what potential people already have inside them is one of the most wonderful aspects of leadership. When this passion is in sync with innate, natural customer service leaders, wonderful things happen.

Your Strongest Customer Service Leader

A brand is defined by the customer's experience.
The experience is delivered by the employees.
-Shep Hyken

Whomever patients ask for by name is your strongest customer service leader. Applaud this, reward this, value this, and let it grow. Put this person in charge of grooming other customer service leaders. Be thankful that you have this customer service superstar on your team.

We have one such customer service superstar at Gorczyca Orthodontics. Her name is Jolene. Jolene has been a dental assistant nearly thirty-eight years. Her dedication is admirable. She has personally trained thirty-six registered dental assistants and serves on the board of Diablo Valley College Dental Assisting Program. She is a tribute to the dental assisting profession.

In a recent Facebook post about Jolene, forty-four patients joined in her praise to thank her for her incredible service. The two most frequent words used to describe Jolene are "awesome" and "amazing." Here is what one patient had to say:

LEADERSHIP

"Jolene is a consummate professional and a pleasure to work with. She is the best and a great asset to the Gorczyca Orthodontics team. She is fabulous!"

How does she do it? Here is what Jolene has to say:

Relationships are the Foundation of Customer Service
Jolene, Registered Dental Assistant for over 38 years

"When I am asked what I love most about work, my answer is the patients. They are what keeps me coming to work each day. I love calling each of them by name, and knowing each one of them individually, their likes and dislikes, their children, their vacations, are all of interest to me.

"I love going out of my way to do things for our patients. Whether it's sending a thank you note, decorating the office, calling to ask how they are, or scheduling an appointment for them in another dental or specialty office, it is always my pleasure to serve the patient and their family in any way that I can. I am thankful that I am able to do this at Gorczyca Orthodontics.

"I enjoy visiting the dental offices in our local community which refer patients to Gorczyca Orthodontics. I am the public relations director for our office, which enables me to visit referring offices several times per year, deliver invitations to team CE events and patient appreciation parties, educational materials, and gifts of appreciation. Over the years, I've made lots of good friends in these offices who I enjoy seeing and catching up with during my visits.

"I love training new dental assistants. Several of these assistants kept in touch with me when no longer at our office. Some of them even call me their second mother! I never planned that things would be this way but being part of dental education has been an important part of my life and career in dentistry. I presently serve on the board of the dental assisting department at the local college, which I attended for my dental assistant training.

"This has been my personal journey of service to my patients, my teammates, Dr. Gorczyca, our community, and the dental profession. It has been a fun trip and I am very thankful for my career in dentistry."

The Leader

If your actions inspire others to dream more, learn more,
do more, and become more, then you are a leader.
-John Quincy Adams

Jim Rohn calls leadership the great challenge of life. As I am writing this book, I reflect on several personal struggles I have had as the leader of my dental team. As a woman dentist, I am challenged to maintain leadership, woman to woman, with the female members of my team, some of whom have more work experience. I need to empower them while maintaining performance and order in my orthodontic office.

As the leader, I must tackle the important problems, bring them to the surface, and find a solution. There are personality traits also, which help create a great leader. The first is to be bold. Address reality. Challenge your team members to do better. Review their management reports. Offer training and education so that interest and expertise can be fostered to build true engagement. Seize the moment to make corrections where mistakes and inefficiencies exist.

While being bold, a leader must also be humble. Humility is a virtue. Admit mistakes not only with the team but with patients, and apologize. Nobody is perfect. This will make you a loved leader and a dentist the team members will want to follow. Humility will enable you to be real.

The leader shares joys and frustrations in the challenges of running a dental office. Team members need to feel they have the freedom to speak openly about what needs to be done to make the office the best that it can be. Transparency and vulnerability build trust. When the truth is always spoken, problems get solved quickly.

Although humble, a leader will also be proud of accomplishments. It takes pride to build an outstanding customer service team. It takes pride to put together an outstanding dental office. It takes pride to educate ourselves, and continue to want to improve. All team members will need to have a sense of pride about their work and what they are providing to their patients. Pride will drive you forward to deliver the best care and service possible.

Leadership requires kindness. Have courage and be kind. There will be times when it will not be easy to be kind to a patient who is mistreating you, insulting you, or taking advantage of you. Always, be professional and be kind. There will be times when frustration will set in with co-workers or team members, but be patient and be kind. Kindness is crucial to having a positive office culture. Kindness of leadership is strength not weakness.

Strength in leadership involves many traits of self-control. Being polite, cool under pressure, and not letting anger get the best of you are essential. To maintain strength in leadership, take a deep breath, and go on.

The leader picks the right people to follow and allows them to succeed. The leader trusts. If the leader does not trust team members and has the continuous need to micromanage or perform "snoopervision" it may be time to assemble a new team. Whatever difficulty you may be facing, take it on, step by step, and lead forward to success.

The Transformational Leader

> *Enjoyment is an incredible energizer to the human spirit.*
> -John C. Maxwell

As we strive to be the world's best dental bosses and providers, we are reminded that it takes more than ourselves to make our dental office successful. Without an excellent team, dentists would not be able to effectively run their dental office. As the leader of the dental team, dentists must inspire teamwork and self-motivation. The leader must provide the tools and education for the team to succeed. As the leader, it will be your purpose to consistently remind your team why their work matters and to refocus them on the true purpose of the dental office—to serve the patient.

An effective leader also knows it's OK to be witty and have a little fun now and then. Take time to laugh. Appropriate humor helps to dissipate tense situations. Humor paves the way to a positive work environment and creates a team bond. Have fun! Your patients will be part of this fun experience and will enjoy your outstanding culture.

Chapter 2

TRUST

*The by-product
of exceptional customer service
is a relationship of trust.*
-Anonymous

Dentist, author, speaker, and business growth coach, David Moffet, author of the book *How to Build the Dental Practice of Your Dreams in Less Than 60 Days Without Killing Yourself* attributes much of his success to the soft skills he learned in dental school working evenings in a Servicemen's Club. There he provided exceptional customer service to his patrons by being friendly and interested in them. He became someone interested in people and somebody people could relate to and trust.

When it comes to building trust with patients, small talk is big talk. Without trust, there is no customer relationship. Without trust, the dental patient will not start treatment. At every opportunity, invest in small talk with your patients. This is a small thing, which is the big thing when it comes to building and maintaining relationships. Nothing is more reassuring, personalized, relaxing, pleasant, or contributory to a sense of trust than casual conversation.

Get your patients talking about themselves. Ask them questions: Where were they born? What are their favorite hobbies? Do they have any children or grandchildren? What are their favorite TV shows and restaurants? What is their favorite sports team? What are their passions? Ask anything that will help you connect with your patients as people.

Perception of Trust

> *Whoever is careless with the truth in small matters cannot be trusted with important matters.*
> -Albert Einstein

TEDx speaker Jim David states that the essence of success in business is relationships. What drives these relationships in business with employees and patients is trust. Trust is the foundation of all relationships. It is our job in dentistry to build trust, grow trust, repair trust, and respect the importance of maintaining trust within our own dental practice.

You want your dental office to be a trusted brand within your community. Like Starbucks, one of the world's most trusted brands, you want members of your community to look forward to coming into your dental office and to say, "We can trust them."

"Trust me, she's a great dentist." As your patients recommend you to others, trust is even more important. Your patients are putting their personal reputation on the line on your behalf when they recommend you. You don't want to let them down.

Trust is greater for individual people than for companies. Take time to highlight the outstanding individuals behind your brand and your customer service. Humanize every interaction. Give every customer service leader their own business card and have their face reflected by a professional portrait on the wall. Encourage your customer service leaders to offer assistance and additional help to all patients. Adopt the one-on-one personalized assistance philosophy whether it be in personal one-on-one communication, by phone, in letters, by e-mail, or on social media.

THREE ELEMENTS OF TRUST

1. ABILITY
2. BENEVOLENCE
3. INTEGRITY

The perception of trust in your dental office is ultimately based on your ability, benevolence, and integrity. All of these factors build the one important thing—trust. What you present to the patient, how you conduct yourself, and how you behave influences the patient's snap judgment. They are thinking, "Should I trust this person? Should I use this dental office? Should I trust this dental team with my dental health, my family's dental health, my referred friend's health?"

ABILITY

Trust is built with consistency.
-Lincoln Chafee

Answering patient's questions well builds trust. Your patient will want proof. They want to know, "Can they do what they say they can do?" To build trust, show Before and After photos of your actual dental treatment. Include a consent agreement for sharing your patient dental records for the education of other patients, teaching purposes, and the public in your initial patient informed consent. Have the patient's name blocked out and written permission given in accordance with HIPAA.

To earn your patient's trust, your patient will need to be educated and reassured about your clinical ability. That is, after all, why they are coming to your dental office—for dental care. Your patients want to know, "Have they done this before?" State and emphasize how many times you have done the clinical procedures they are seeking, for how long, and your rate of success. Share patient testimonials in an effort to build new patient confidence. Demonstrate study models of completed cases. Inform them of your years in practice, specialist training, and special skills. Introduce the new patient to your trusted team. Emphasize individual team member longevity.

Complete an office tour. Emphasize safety, cleanliness, comfort, and friendliness. Let them know how long you have been in practice, and emphasize your commitment to the community.

Once achieved, preserve and respect your patient's trust. If you are a dental specialist, make sure your patients are informed of your training. If you are not a dental specialist and performing specialist procedures, be truthful. There is no faster way to lose a patient than to say, "As of last weekend, I've started doing orthodontics." Refer to a specialist for a specialist consultation. Always tell the truth. This is especially true when something goes wrong.

Certainly, things don't always go as planned in dentistry. Be truthful about all situations, apologize, and make it right. If your dental office violates a patient's trust, it is a customer service killer. Trust will be lost and the patient will think twice before doing business with you again.

Author and businessman Dave Kerpen, in his book *Likeable Business* writes of the benefits of being human when building patient trust. When small mishaps happen, admit your office made a mistake and move on. Customers want to feel like they're interacting with a genuine and honest person, not a machine or a cold, soulless company.

When you are personal with your patients, they will be personal towards you. Both dental office customer service leaders and the patients will feel comfortable expressing their true feelings and personality when there is trust. When trust is present, your dental office will be the "go-to dental location" and patients will have a high level of personal comfort and engagement.

Benevolence

Good leaders must first become good servants.
-Robert K. Greenleaf

Business is behavior. Trust begins with caring for the other person. This is known as benevolence. Benevolence puts the other person first. It is built on integrity, honesty, and transparency. It is created by responsiveness to our customers in the delivery of their care. In medicine and dentistry, it is also built on the oath "Do no harm." In this way, we build patient trust. Putting others ahead of ourselves is the essence of serving others and the foundation of outstanding customer service.

Ultimately in the business model, the behavior of benevolence leads to prosperity in the service industry of dentistry. Benevolence is the foundation of the service mindset and the serviced attitude. It is serving with humility. The business of dentistry is about the thriving patient and always putting the patient first.

Caring deeply on a personal level counts. It is the foundation of benevolence, caring for another person more than ourselves. Benevolence is the core of the statement, "We will take great care of you." It's the basis of outstanding customer service.

Your patient is continuously asking themselves, "Does my dentist care about me?" For the answer to this question to be "Yes," our actions must be purely in the best interests of the patient. If you have the ability to do great dentistry and refer your patient to other great specialists for the highest quality of comprehensive dental care possible, but you don't because you are driven by ego or money, you will be perceived as untrustworthy. Your patients could even grow to fear you and mistrust the dental profession.

The majority of customers interact with a dental office with confidence over the smallest of things. When patients trust you with the smallest things they will trust you with the biggest thing, their healthcare. This is especially true with a $40,000 interdisciplinary smile makeover. This is a team effort, and patient trust needs to exist for every member of the dental team.

Patient trust starts at the initial phone call. This patient already trusts you enough to visit your office. It may be due to trust built through word-of-mouth referral or by the educational marketing materials which you have produced. If trust is maintained or built during the first call, your new patient will proceed to an initial exam. Trust grows during the diagnosis and presentation of the treatment plan. A diagnostic wax-up of the proposed treatment and introduction of the interdisciplinary team builds stronger trust. Finally, trust is solidified with the comprehensive treatment plan and delivery of dental services. In order to build patient trust, you must demonstrate ability for getting the job done in a doable, affordable, comfortable, and timely manner.

The ultimate reflection of level of trust is reflected by your present customers, your patients, recommending you to others—their family and friends. Master trust through your actions and letting the patient know that, "We will take great care of you."

Integrity

> *To give real service you must add something*
> *which cannot be bought or measured with money,*
> *and that is sincerity and integrity.*
> -Douglas Adams

The foundation of integrity is doing what you say you will do, and delivering what you have promised to deliver. Your brand will continue to prove itself by completion of dental treatment and delivery of great customer service. The integrity exhibited by doing what you say you will do and delivering what you promise to deliver builds customer trust and office reputation in the community.

With long-term employees, there is not only trust but also respect with the performance proof of integrity. Long-term employees are empowered and confident. There is a mutual respect, ownership, and participation in office decision-making processes. Empowered employees can usually solve problems on the spot for the customer. There's a level of confidence which comes with the knowledge that you can say yes to resolve a patient situation because your employer will back up your decision and actions to do so. This is mutual trust for the benefit of customer service. It's what we work towards as owners of dental offices. To have empowered team members, serving patients, and putting patients first.

Trusted employees will always speak highly of their office. Trusted employees are critical in the recruitment and maintenance of other great team members. Things which diminish patient trust are discord, poor management, firing, and lay-off. Try to avoid these situations. If impossible, be honest, open, and transparent about the situation and inform everyone opening about what is going on or what needs to happen. Surprises diminish trust. This safety and security allows employees to have a high degree of focus on their number one job priority of patient care.

Keep a level of camaraderie and light humor to maintain happiness and foster trust and loyalty with the team. Happiness through trust will better motivate your employees to truly love what they do, where they work, and make your customer service the very best that it can be.

Doctor Trust

Trust is the glue of life.
It's the most essential ingredient in effective communication.
It's the foundational principle that holds all relationships.
                                        -Stephen Covey

Communication is key to building trust in the dentist-patient relationship. Patients need to be truthfully told everything regarding their dental condition and choices. Both parties need to listen effectively. The patient needs to be active in the decision-making process and know that their best interests are always maintained by the dentist. When this is done, dental trust is built.

Trust is a two-way street. In order for patients to trust the doctor, the doctor must always tell the truth, act ethically, demonstrate ability, benevolence, and integrity, and also trust the patient.

In the dentist-patient relationship, trust is built by the assurance that personal information is confidential, procedures are in the patient's best interest, and that patient autonomy is recognized. Patients have more trust and confidence in dentists who communicate well with compassion. In the end, clear communication builds not only trust, but reduces patient anxiety and fear of the dental procedures. Ultimately, your patient's trust and confidence will determine whether they will seek treatment in your dental office.

To build patient trust, patients expect dentists to listen and understand their feelings and needs. Ever since the Patient Bill of Rights, patients have been encouraged to participate more in their treatment plan decisions. Research has shown that some patients do not desire more involvement in the decision-making process, while others want to learn more about their treatment plan and want an active role in the process. Research has shown that patients with higher trust tend to be less active while those who feel less trust for their dentist tend to take a more active role in the treatment plan decision-making process. In order to engender trust, dentists need to maintain an egalitarian relationship with their patients rather than a paternalistic one. This can be achieved by involving the patient as much as possible in the decision-making process.

Studies have shown that patients tend to seek out healthcare providers with whom they share a similar ethnic background with whom they already have an inherently higher level of trust. Kindness and compassion build trust. Listening builds trust. Presenting honest and ethical treatment opinions to patients in a caring manner builds trust through clear and effective communication.

Dentists will often be offering honest opinions and second opinions. It is important that this always be done in the patient's best interest with fairness and truthfulness. The longer and more thorough the consultation, the more likely that mutual trust in the dentist-patient relationship is achieved.

Shared decision-making builds trust. A three-step process can be utilized to discover what is important to the patient, in order to arrive at the best treatment decision.

1. Simply ask and determine what is important to the patient.
2. Offer options and discuss risks and benefits with the patient.
3. Set achievable goals, together with the patient.

The Press-Ganey customer service survey in medicine, which provides patient satisfaction feedback, asks the important question, "Did the doctor share the decision-making process with you?" Let's all aim to score 100% on this question with our dental patients.

Team Member Trust

*The achievement of an organization is the result
of a combined effort of every individual.*
-Vince Lombardi

Sir Richard Branson of Virgin America Airlines states that the customer service experience is everything in business. It begins with the employees of the business. Beyond the owner, employees are the greatest asset of any business. They need to be empowered by a positive work environment and have an innately good outlook on life. They must be proud of their company that is focused on continuous quality improvement in order to give outstanding customer service. They must be nurtured to have a passion and commitment for serving the customer. In order to achieve all of these things, team members must trust the company and the company must trust them.

In an atmosphere of trust there will be more efficiency, production, creativity, fulfillment, laughter, and happiness. When team members develop a deep sense of trust in each other, their workplace, and the doctor, they feel the freedom to let down their own guard, thereby being better able to focus fully on serving the customer. In the presence of trust, your office culture will be one of joy and purpose. This high level of trust will not only carry over to your outstanding customer service team, but it will also be the foundation of your organization and the core of your company. Here customer service innovation happens.

Lack of team member trust produces a need for "micromanagement." This is a fast way to drive away customers and also to lose other employees. If management does not trust a member of the service team, why should patients? We need a commitment from our work force that only the truth shall be spoken through actions and words. Untrustworthiness cannot be tolerated on a team of customer service leaders. Once trust in a team member is lacking, or absent, it is doubtful that it can be rebuilt and not forgotten. It may be best to cut your losses with due cause, and eliminate the team member who is dragging down your office culture, care, and climate in order to rebuild your customer service dream team.

Take time to care for the openness of your team through communication and improvement of customer service systems and processes. Educational events, cross-trainings, and social gatherings of your team build trust. Look for ways to affirm and build up your employees. Give compliments and appreciation for jobs well done.

Remember to keep the office conversation appropriate to topics reflecting your excellent customer service culture, care, and climate when patients are present. Broken equipment, schedule changes, and other business operational aspects of your daily schedule are off limits for open discussion when patients are present.

To keep the customer service culture, care, and climate enjoyable, offer critique or "suggestions" for improvement to team members in private and not openly in front of patients. Praise in public, and criticize in private. Praise and appreciation go a long way in building your customer service team morale and focus. Keep the positivity of great customer service flowing.

Chapter 3

OWNERSHIP

We are what we repeatedly do.
Excellence then is not an act but a habit.
-Aristotle

We have a saying at our office, "If I see it, I own it." It is our mantra of ownership of the customer service experience. When ownership exists, there is a very strong customer service bond between ourselves and our customers. Everyone in your dental office owns the patient experience. There will be minor mistakes, actions, and systems that will need continual correction. What we don't want is an environment of blame and excuses. When something goes wrong, a customer service leader takes corrective action. We don't make excuses, blame others, or look for a way out of the situation. We take personal responsibility to solve the problem immediately.

Ownership describes individual responsibility for creation of a great patient experience. The quality of patient care is reflected by the level of ownership of each member. Reflection of this ownership is in the statement, "When I see a problem, I own it. The problem will be resolved by me. I will see the problem through to a solution. I want to give our patients immediate service in the present moment. When I receive a request, I own it, discuss it, resolve it, so that it will be better for the patient at this time as well as all patients the next time."

Patients deserve seasoned professionals. The response, "I'm new here" cannot be given as an antidote for failed customer service. When in a bind, try the responses, "Let me look into that," or "Let me resolve this." Don't forget to say, "I'd be happy to help you."

Ownership Questions

Ownership is based on individual actions and accountability. To measure ownership, try asking these questions:

1. Did I do my best?
2. Did I make progress?
3. Did I build a positive relationship?
4. Was I fully engaged?

Marshall Goldsmith, in his book *Triggers,* lists engagement questions such as these that teach ownership. Team members are more likely to go the extra mile when they feel that they have ownership in the customer service experience.

Glitches, which will occur in your patient care systems, need to be discussed at team meetings and eliminated. Document repeat customer service successes and eliminate failures. Put systems and processes in place so that oversights and mishaps do not happen again. When mistakes do happen, make a personal commitment to assure that they don't happen again. This is true ownership.

Initial Welcome

A smile is the universal welcome.
-Max Eastman

"Hi! My name is Pam. I spoke with you on the phone. Welcome to our office. How's your morning been so far?"

Friendliness begins at your first point of contact with the new patient. It may be on the phone. It may be at the front door. It may be at the front desk. Wherever and whenever it is, take time to get to know your patient, listen to their needs and concerns, ask them questions about themselves and their day, and show that you care. You only get one chance to make a good first impression.

When the new patient arrives, it will take about three seconds for them to make a snap judgment about you, your dental office, and the level of care you provide. Every good interaction starts with a warm, sincere, and authentic greeting. Be prepared. You want that first impression to be memorable.

The receptionist seated closest to the door is the welcome "concierge" waiting for the new patient to arrive. Whoever has this important job must be fast on their feet, ready to stand, shake hands, and say, "Welcome to our office, we're so glad you are here," in a sincere, positive, and friendly manner.

To accomplish and give importance to this goal, think of your front desk as the customer service emergency room. Your concierge will be your first responder. Your EMT or ER nurse will be gathering data to determine how much attention and customer service care your new patient needs. The most important aspect of this first interaction is that the patient is welcomed and does not wait to be seen. The new patient and their family are the most important people in your dental universe.

Have you ever seen a limousine driver at the airport waiting for their client with a little sign with the client's name? The sign reads, "Mr. Jones." It means "I'm here for you." We all walk past these men at the airport and we wish there would be someone there with our name on a sign making us feel important and cared for. This is the meaningful and heartfelt feeling you can give your new patient in your dental office with a personalized welcome sign. You may even want to have your welcome sign transferred to the exam room. Your goal is to have your new patient and their family feel special throughout their entire encounter to feel your constant presence; starting with sentiments such as "Welcome," "Great to see you today," and "Thanks for coming in," goes a long way to meeting this customer service expectation.

The Initial Phone Call

First impressions matter.
Experts say we size up new people in somewhere
between thirty seconds and two minutes.
-Elliot Abrams

Here is practical advice to share with your team. We all know the Batman hotline, a red phone that is always answered immediately. Have your team give this kind of attention to your new patient phone call. Answer calls with enthusiasm within three rings. Listen to your patient and don't be distracted by your computer. Do not multi-task at this critical time. Take handwritten notes. Otherwise, it is highly likely that as you type, your voice will start to sound like a robot.

Is there a smile on the face of your receptionist when she answers the phone? "Hello, Mrs. Jones, this is Pam. We are so happy that you have called! How may I help you today? I'm happy to schedule that appointment for you. We're looking forward to seeing you."

Take time to schmooze. Get to know the new caller. Listen and get to know one another. Imagine it's a blind date and you're hoping to start a relationship.

The last thing a new patient needs to hear is, "click, click, click" while you ask the new patient to repeat or speak more slowly. You don't want to sound like the drive-through clerk taking orders at a fast-food joint.

Have colored sheets with scripted questions. There's no need to read the questions word-for-word. Use the questions as a guide. Questions help you touch upon every category of information needed to get to know the new patient.

You may also want to have a different colored sheet for Spanish-speaking phone calls. In California, it is essential to have a Spanish-speaking receptionist. Survey your community and decide what additional languages you may need to accommodate.

Should anyone come within talking distance of the new patient phone call, hold the colored paper up as a "Do not disturb" sign. Once the phone call is completed, enter pertinent information into the computer. This strategy will free up your mind and listening skills during the call allowing you to give your full, undivided attention to the new calls.

Prioritize your gathering of information. Number one is the new patient's phone number. Next is the new patient's name. Third, schedule the new exam appointment. After you have these three things accomplished, you can schmooze. But keep focused until you are sure to have your critical information.

Phone Etiquette

*Etiquette is the science of living.
It embraces everything.
It is honor.*
-Emily Post

It is important to review with your team good phone and verbal etiquette. When answering the phone, always ask, "May I place you on hold?" before ever putting a caller on hold. If the new caller says "No," ask the patient at the front desk to kindly wait while the phone call is completed.

Use the caller's name. Thank them for calling. Do not screen calls. Strive to eliminate voice messages and call transfers as much as possible.

Morning and Lunchtime Phone Service

Many working individuals make phone calls in the early morning and during lunchtime. A recent review of call tracking in our office revealed that most new patient calls were made between 8 a.m. and 9 a.m. and noon to 1:00 p.m. It is essential that the phones be answered during the lunch hour. Divide the lunch period between two receptionists so that the phones are always answered. Also, schedule an early morning receptionist to take calls during commute hours.

In terms of lunch, remember that you are always there to serve your patients. Avoid talking about your lunch break in front of the patient. Focus on the patient in front of you. To avoid focusing on time, do not have wall clocks in patient areas. Never rush patients and always remain calm.

After School Phone Service

Answer the phones until 5:00 p.m. or closing time. You may want to continue answering your phones until 5:30 p.m., as team members finish up for the day. This is especially important on Friday afternoons when parents have a few free moments and start thinking about children's needs for the weekend. This static will reduce weekend calls and emergencies.

Voicemail

David Moffet, creator of the Ultimate Patient Experience, and his wife, Jayne Bandy, CEO and Founder of Dental Phone Excellence, recommend that the phone always be answered even with patients standing at the front desk. They recommend that in just a few moments, the caller's name, phone number, and reason for call can be known, and they can be called back immediately if needed. The Moffets suggest that the patient waiting at the front desk will appreciate that when they call the office you will likewise answer the phone promptly, offering service in an efficient manner.

There will be times when all available front desk personnel are busy with patients and callers, and voice message is unavoidable. These calls need to be returned as quickly as possible, as, for example, the caller who wants to inform you that they are stuck in traffic and will be a few minutes late.

Voicemail needs to be checked several times per day to insure that no calls are missed. If necessary, block dedicated time to ensure that messages are not left for hours unanswered. Just as the front desk receptionist probably collects the mail at a certain time of the day, have them check voicemail regularly, at planned times. A possible routine could be 8:30 a.m., 11:30 a.m., 1:30 p.m., and 4:30 p.m.

After-Hours Calls

You may want to hire an answering service so that no calls go to voicemail after hours. This practice is very common with oral surgery offices that receive many emergency calls. In orthodontics and general dentistry, it is not uncommon to leave the doctor's personal cell phone number on the answering machine.

Pagers tend to elicit more late night calls than leaving a personal cell phone number. Years ago, we had office pagers and it was not uncommon for patients to call Friday night at 11:30 p.m. to say that their retainer or aligner was not fitting. When the pager call was returned by the doctor, the patient was surprised because they were expecting an answering service. Personally, I think leaving the doctor's cell phone number on the answering machine is a great sign of customer service that patients appreciate and respect, without abusing the privilege.

Scheduling

There cannot be a crisis next week.
My schedule is already full.
                        -Henry A. Kissinger

In dentistry, emergencies and delays are inevitable. Most patients are understanding and forgiving. An accurate estimate of wait time helps immensely. Accompany the announcement of a wait time with an apology. Offer a refreshment, a magazine, or TV entertainment. Show respect for your patient and their family. Value their time and appreciate their business.

At Disneyland, the sign reads "45 minute wait until ride time." Yet the crowd remains happy and looks forward to the ride with anticipation. Disneyland is the happiest place on earth. At Disneyland, delays are always expressed. There is no guessing. When wait time is admitted and communicated, there will be less stress and upset. Under promise and over deliver.

We in dentistry can all learn something from the customer service leaders at Disneyland, where associates greet visitors warmly and welcome them to the park. Videos and announcements provide pleasant distractions during a wait line. There are many similar activities in the dental office reception area to entertain for a short bit of time. Offer your customers a magazine and a fresh cup of tea or coffee or other beverage. Ask if they would like to watch what is playing on TV or prefer to change the channel. Kids can play video games. Aromatic candles can be lit, water fountains run, or even hand massages given. Be sure to have comfortable furniture in your reception area. Have the room clean and fragrant.

Years ago, I did not have a flat screen TV in my reception area. If there were more than a five minute wait, patients and their families would immediately come to the front desk and inquire how much longer it would be until their appointment. The reception area was loud and active. After we added a flat screen TV, the transformation was remarkable. Suddenly, everyone was calm. The room was quiet, and everyone sat comfortably, watching TV. No one approached the front desk in anticipation of their appointment. Some patients were actually disappointed when it was time for their treatment because they wanted to continue watching TV. It was a miracle!

There will be a time when you will need to communicate to a patient that there will be a wait. Train your front-line team member to recognize and address wait time. Experienced receptionists and dental assistants can mitigate effects of a delay. Communication is key. Setting the expectation of wait time psychologically prepares the customer for what is to follow.

When dealing with parents who might be dropping off and picking up children at several locations, ask, "Are you able to wait or should we reschedule your appointment?" The customer then has options. Let your customer make the choice as to whether they would like to wait and be seen or prefer to reschedule. Always do what is best for the customer.

Have you ever been to a restaurant that gave you the wait time with a pager? Were you upset? Most probably, you were not. It is likely that you thought, *Wow, this is a great restaurant!* It can be the same for you in your dental office. Handled properly, waiting patients can take a walk, visit the restroom, get a snack, or even shop next door if they know the length of time delay. It is a common courtesy to give people the heads-up on when they can expect to be seen.

If the patient has waited unnecessarily, you may want to give a small token of service recovery. This could range anywhere from a heartfelt apology to a $5 gift card from Starbucks. Your ultimate goal is to exceed your patient's expectations.

RUNNING LATE

> *Patience is not simply the ability to wait—*
> *it's how we behave while we're waiting*
> -Joyce Meyer

The friendly dental assistant greets the patient and says, "The doctor is finishing up an emergency surgical procedure. The wait time may be thirty minutes. Are you willing and able to wait or would you like to reschedule?" Yet when the patient is seated, the wait time was only fifteen minutes. The patient thinks, *Wow! This office is great! I only waited fifteen minutes!*

Now imagine if the assistant had told the patient, "It will be just a few minutes." A few minutes is perceived as three to nine minutes. The patient waits fifteen minutes. They start to think now that the wait may be half an hour. Anxiety builds. Trust begins to be lost. This wait now produces disappointing results. They are upset that they have waited fifteen minutes.

Disney manages wait time every day. People wait in line and are totally happy. Disney under promises and over delivers.

Nothing will kill the customer experience faster than running late. Prepare not to run late and always seat the patient on time. Having an additional treatment chair ensures that the patient will be seated on time. This helps the patient feel that the wait is over. The patient now has a little extra time to relax and read their favorite magazine.

No matter what you do, because of unexpected emergencies or lengthy/difficult procedures, there will be a time when you will run late. Communicate the wait. Manage the wait time effectively.

My husband is a very busy cancer surgeon. His team offers to schedule urgent patients on the next available office day. They tell the patient, "There will be a very long wait but the doctor will see you as soon as possible. Please bring a lunch. Please bring a book. We will give you a pager. Feel free to walk around. Expect to be here all day. We will page you when it is time for your appointment." What amazes me is that my husband's cancer patients are rarely upset. They bring him gifts as tokens of their appreciation, to thank him for his service. I've often wondered if frank communication is the cause of their generosity or if happiness is produced by slowing down and deciding to enjoy life to the fullest at this time with the removal of the importance or perception that life is running late.

Doctor Time

Attention All Doctors: Be on time! This includes arriving on time in the morning, returning from lunch promptly, and avoiding electronic distractions. Beware of the evils of unnecessary e-mails and social media, where seconds of "just checking" turn into minutes of delays. I have a secret for you: these are your team's and patient's pet peeves!

Respect your patient's time. If you have a busy mother with several children waiting for one child's dental appointment to be completed, let her know how long the treatment will take. She may want to leave one child at the office, leave to pick another up at school, and return back to the office.

New patients, in particular, must not wait. New exams are the lifeblood of your practice. They are your number one priority. The doctor treatment coordinator should serve the new patient first when making scheduling and management decisions. Concentrate on delivering a great first impression.

THANK YOU

Take time to be kind and to say "Thank you."
-Zig Ziglar

Make gratitude part of your office culture, care, and climate. Be thankful for your patients and the business that they provide. This habit solidifies the doctor-patient relationship. Take time to express your sincere thanks either verbally or in writing.

In this electronic age, do not underestimate the impact of a heartfelt handwritten Thank You note sent by Snail Mail to your patient in appreciation of their loyalty, treatment completion, or special kindness. Extending sincere, old-fashioned gratitude in a written note has an esteemed place among high-touch practices. The arrival of a beautiful note or card by mail can be a joyous surprise, keeping your office and customer service experience top of mind.

NON-DOCTOR DAYS

When the doctor is away, the doors stay unlocked and the lights on during normal business hours. It's business as usual at the front desk. This includes maintaining the dress code and not eating on the job. It's just as if the doctor were present on non-doctor working days. Patients will walk in at all times to make appointments. Anyone working in the dental office needs to look smart and be sharp at all times to make a good first impression.

On non-doctor working days, the phone should be answered just as if the doctor were present. If your office will not be staffed, you may want to use a phone answering service such as Dental Support Specialties so that your phone can still be answered by a human being. You can find them at www.dentalsupportspecialties.com.

CROSS-TRAINING

There is only one boss: the customer.
And he can fire everyone in the company from the chairman
on down, simply by spending his money somewhere else.
-Sam Walton

Nothing kills customer service faster than being understaffed. Attendance is critical for an excellent team delivering five-star customer care. All team members and especially the doctor need to practice a good work ethic of excellent attendance and of being on time.

"That's not my job," "That's not our policy," "You need to talk to someone else," and "I didn't do it" are responses that should never be heard in the dental office. In my book, *Beyond the Morning Huddle: HR Management for a Successful Dental Office*, I describe the importance of cross-training and the benefits of team members being able to perform as many jobs as possible, if not all jobs, in the dental office. Outstanding customer service is a central part of everyone's primary job.

Tell the Patient What You CAN DO for Them, Not What You Can't Do
Veronica, RDA, Treatment Coordinator

"Every day in the orthodontic office is different. Every family is special, and every patient is unique. To me, that's what customer service is all about, individualized attention.

"I love working with new patients and their families, answering their questions about how orthodontics can solve their dental and bite problems, and giving them the beautiful smile they desire. Start to finish, I love coordinating the patient's orthodontic journey.

"Customer service is noble selflessness. We are here to serve the patient. I love helping the patient in an efficient yet friendly manner. I assure the patient what I CAN DO for them, to serve their needs, in the best way possible. Everything is negotiable. We want to make orthodontic treatment possible for every patient that we serve.

"Consider when a patient tells you 'I can't afford ideal dental care,' that they are actually saying, 'Show me how I can afford the dental care I deserve.' Tell the patient what you CAN DO to make treatment possible for them, not what you can't do. Sooner or later, you will come to a workable solution and a financial arrangement to start treatment.

"What customer service means to me is treating each new patient like family. To take excellent care of our patients, excellent attendance of the entire team is necessary. We cannot perform our own jobs confidently if we are one person

down or covering for an absent team member. Attendance is critical. We need team members we can count on and trust to provide outstanding patient care.

"It is my responsibility to give new patients a prompt response to their questions and help them through the treatment process, especially when getting started. We do this by many forms of communication: calling, text messaging, e-mailing, as well as personal mail. We want our office and doctor to be our patient's family orthodontist for life. Once you are our patient, we want to maintain our relationship with you even after the orthodontic treatment is completed.

"We take time to get to know each patient personally from the first moment they step foot into our office. At each new exam, Dr. Gorczyca begins by getting to know the patient and asking questions and listening. We have a welcome sign in the exam room with the new patient's name. Dr. Gorczyca first asks, 'What can we do to get you to love your smile?' We always start with the patient's desires and we give the patient the opportunity to express themselves.

"'What questions do you have for me?' is something I say dozens of times each day. I take time with each patient to answer all of their questions.

"We let each patient know, 'We will take great care of you.' We guarantee satisfaction. Nothing gives us more pleasure then seeing our patients' beautiful smiles. In today's busy world, patients need help prioritizing time and activities. That's what I'm here to do. Prioritize their orthodontic treatment.

"There can never be too much communication with patients. Customer service is what I love most about my job as a treatment coordinator at Gorczyca Orthodontics."

Chapter 4

COMMUNICATION

*Service is not a list of off-the-shelf solutions.
It's a constant process of discovery.
To be of real service, one must be willing to constantly
discover exactly what the customer wants or needs—
and then provide it.*
-Mark Ursino

You drive up to the guard and your name is checked on the VIP guest list. As you open your car door and get out of your car, the valet and bellmen who are expecting you, welcome you, and greet you by name. The front desk concierge has similarly started to prepare your personalized greeting. Well-dressed attendees are walking around looking, listening, and constantly communicating by tiny earphones like secret agents of customer service. Their mission is five-star customer service. They're ready, they're able, and they're keeping notes. This is your arrival at a five-star resort.

Positive and effective communication is the foundation of great customer service. Attention and consistency are key. There is no unimportant employee, conversation, or task when it comes to customer service. Each customer contact is an important touchpoint moment. Every word, every touch, and every act of kindness counts. Everyone on the customer service team must strive to build a memorable customer service experience. Attention and consistency of communication are keys to your customer service success.

COMMUNICATION

The Initial Phone Call

*Thirty-two percent of calls that go to an answering message
or are placed on hold hang up and don't call back.*
-Jayne Bandy

Answering calls quickly, within three rings, by a likeable, social person, is essential to great customer service. Create a system to ensure that the caller's name and phone number are politely collected. Only then has your initial phone call achieved success.

The success of the initial phone call can by determined by call tracking. In the state of California, calls may not be recorded before first telling the caller, "This call will be recorded for training purposes." I have only found one company that does call tracking with voice recording well for a very inexpensive price—Valpak. For $25 per month, you can have all your new patient calls tracked through their service and sent to a special number. These call times, conversational details, and conversion rate into new starts can be studied for the purpose of improvement.

Call tracking will reveal many important things about customer calls. When do most new patients call? Was the call answered within three rings within normal business hours or was it missed? Do new callers hang-up? Do new callers wait on the line while the receptionist finishes another call? How long are new callers willing to wait? Was your receptionist polite? Did she get the most important information in the appropriate order? Was the information correct? Did her voice sound pleasant? Was she friendly? Did the new patient, after the call, follow through, making and keeping the initial exam appointment?

Test your own phone service. Call your office and listen. Check your phone answering systems daily. What you find may surprise you. I usually call my own office on my way to work and also on days that I am not working. Phone service providers are constantly going out of order or experiencing minor difficulties. You need to stay on top of what is going on with the phone lines and Internet service in your own local community.

No phone service is perfect. During one malfunction, the phone company placed a message "This number is no longer in service!" You can image my reaction to this inappropriate message! We switched back to another carrier. You will need to test services in your own area to find which is superior.

Your messaging system can include when the patient can expect to hear back from you. If it is during the active work day state, "Your call will be returned within four hours." During a work week night, the message system should state, "Your message will be answered within twenty-four hours." If it is on the weekend state, "Your call will be returned on Monday morning at 8:30 a.m." Longer delays may lead customers to conclude that you're not that interested in their business.

Before a receptionist at your front desk ends a new patient call, it is important she ask, "Is there anything else I can help you with today?" and "Are there any additional family members who would like to be seen for an initial consultation?" Asking questions is the best way to offer help. Say thank you to the new patient for calling your office. Confirmation of the new patient appointment day, date, and time will solidify the meeting agreement. Being friendly, tell your new patient that everyone at the office is looking forward to seeing them. This will help make your new caller feel welcomed and create the feeling of belonging at your office prior to their first appointment.

Your Concierge

We serve our customers as invited guests to a party, and we are the hosts.
-Jeff Bezos

She is perhaps the most influential team member in your dental office: the front-line receptionist. As your front door concierge, your receptionist is your face of customer service. She sits closest to the front door. Her highest priority is to meet and greet the new patient. She makes or breaks the first impression of your office brand.

You concierge can offer new patients an office tour. In my first book, *It All Starts with Marketing*, I list the twelve steps of an office tour. As the concierge walks about with the new patient, team members will take the time to say hello with a friendly smile. The new patient will be evaluating your office and everyone in it. They will be using their five senses to form a final impression of your office and their new patient experience.

Three Steps of Customer Service

I have learned to imagine an invisible sign around each person's neck that says 'Make me feel important.'
-Mary Kay Ash

Your communication style will convey your level of in-office, face-to-face customer service. Consider three steps of patient focus.

STEP 1. WELCOME

Greet the patient by name. Ask, "How is your day going?" Stop and listen. Ask questions. Take your time.

Most times the patient will respond and then politely ask, "How are you today?" Try using the response "FANTASTIC!," no matter what kind of day you are having. Make it a fantastic day for both you and your patient.

Excellent customer service communication includes positivity. Your patient does not want to hear "I'm sick," "I'm tired," or "I was late for work." Don't be a Debbie Downer! Leave your personal problems at the office front door. Focus on your top priority: the patient. Here are six positive responses to choose from to help you make it a great day:

1. FANTASTIC!
2. Awesome!
3. Outstanding!
4. Great!
5. Excellent!
6. Very well, thank you

Your job is to make it a great day for your patient. You will find that you make it an even better day for yourself in the process.

STEP 2. SERVING NEEDS

Whether emotional or dental, serve your patients' needs. Ask, "How are you doing?" Discuss the progress of their dental health. Make your patient feel great. Give them a smile.

Every team member will need to be empowered to serve the patient quickly and immediately. Adopt the philosophy "If I see it, hear it, or I receive it, I own it," for immediate satisfaction of the patients' needs.

STEP 3. THANK YOU AND FOND FAREWELL

Thank each patient individually for choosing your office and for referring their family and friends. Shake your patient's hand and give them a thank you pat on the shoulder. With younger patients or during flu season, try a fist bump. Tell your patient that you look forward to seeing them again next time.

Your goodbye will be the last memory of your office in the heart and mind of your patient until the next time. Give a fond farewell. You may want to embellish this final experience with an invitation to a Patient Appreciation Party or by telling your patient that you would love to have more patients just like them. Allow time to say goodbye and tell your patient that you are looking forward to seeing them again next time.

FOUR RULES OF COMMUNICATION

1. LISTEN

> *We have two ears and one mouth so that we can*
> *listen twice as much as we speak.*
> *-Epictetus*

First listen. When you listen, you will discover what is important to your patient. They will tell you what they want, how they want it, and when they want it. Listen well so your patients know that you care about them. Active listening is your primary customer service communication. Listen to the details of what your patients say.

Watch and listen intensely to what is happening with your patients at every touchpoint. Gather customer feedback and act on it. Constantly gather non-verbal cues, patient comments, and written feedback, starting TODAY, in order to foster a healthy, productive environment.

ACTIVE LISTENING

Dental patients come to us for many reasons. They want to be heard. They would like to receive attention during their patient care journey.

If you come to Gorczyca Orthodontics, any weekday morning, you will mostly encounter women receiving treatment of braces or Invisalign. Of course, there are a few men and a few children, but in general, these populations do not seek orthodontic treatment in the morning. Women want their teeth straight. So, after they drop their kids off at school and go to the gym, they head directly to the orthodontist's office.

Many women seeking orthodontic treatment may have gone for multiple opinions before choosing the location for their orthodontic care. Women ages forty to sixty are the most demanding population. They are probably also the most prevalent morning customers. How could you fill your office with these new patients? Be willing to listen.

DON'T INTERRUPT

Listening is not simply hearing the words that are spoken.
Listening is understanding why the words were spoken.
-Simon Sinek

Counselors and therapists listen intently when they practice "active listening." This skill requires patience. One aspect of active listening is to hear everything the other person has to say, without interruption. Even if there is a pause, don't interject. Hear your patient out until he or she is completely drained and has nothing more to say. Ask, "Is there anything more I can do for you today?" Let them answer until they are done.

I know what you are thinking. *This active listening will take so much time in my office that it will interfere with my schedule and production.* Active listening is difficult for dentists. But patients are generally respectful of the doctor's time. And, active listening is not limited to the doctor. It is a whole team goal. You may even want to appoint an active listener coordinator to be in charge of listening, while the rest of the team and doctor keep the office schedule flowing.

SHOW YOU ARE LISTENING

Active listening includes eye contact. Too little eye contact is viewed negatively. Lack of eye contact can convey a lack of interest, inattention, or trust. It may even be viewed as deceptive. So, sit down, pull your chair out in front of your dental patient, and look them in the eyes.

In this digital age, it is more important than ever to make eye contact. Ask yourself, "What color are my patient's eyes?" If you can answer this one question, you can be sure that you have made sound eye contact during your conversation.

Respond to your patient's feelings. Nod your head in understanding and camaraderie. You may not always agree with your patient, but expressing you care will provide empathy no matter what they are going through.

PARAPHRASE WHAT YOUR CUSTOMER HAS SAID

Repeat to confirm what your patient has expressed to you to confirm what they are trying to communicate. You want to make sure that your understanding of the patient's wants and needs is correct. This is your opportunity to be not only a good communicator, but a great communicator. Make suggestions for treatment and care based upon what the patient has said. Build self-esteem during the conversation. Be active and proactive. Whatever you do at this point in the communication process, do not sit silently.

The words "I understand" are two of the most caring words anyone can ever speak. Communicate your understanding. These words produce a bond. You may say, "Tell me more about that," if you need further clarification.

Be sure to use positive responses like, "FANTASTIC!," "My pleasure," and, "I would be happy to." "Wonderful," "Great," and "Thank you" always make others feel appreciated and confident. Other positive responses include "You're welcome," "Certainly," "Good morning," "Good afternoon," "Good evening," and "I appreciate you so much." Never forget to say "Please," and "Thank you," not only to your patients, but also to your team of service leaders.

Try active listening every day with every customer. Soon, it will become ingrained in you and your office culture. Then, active listening will be there when it is most needed, that one day when you come into contact with an unhappy patient.

2. BE POLITE

You can be strong
and true to yourself
without being rude or loud.
          -Paula Radcliffe

Even if you are understaffed, your equipment is malfunctioning, you're having the worst day of your life, or the patient is driving you into an emotional state of frenzy, you must maintain professional control of your temperament and never be rude. There is no excuse for ever being anything less than polite in a professional service environment.

There must be zero tolerance for rudeness. Team members are impolite for one reason: the leader, the practice owner, dentist, or supervising manager allows this behavior. You hired wrong, trained wrong, or coached wrong. Now you have a serious problem. If you allow this behavior to exist, customers will be lost.

3. HAVE EMOTIONAL CONTROL

Is the customer always right? No, but make it your goal to make the patient "feel" right. Your customer is your highest priority and their happiness is your success.

During the most difficult customer service situations, always put the patient first ahead of your own feelings. This is your role as customer service leader. Stay prepared for when dealing with a conversation becomes difficult. Hear the customer's side of the story. Don't get defensive and don't take what an unhappy patient may say in your dental office personally. Take action to make things right for the customer.

4. TAKE ACTION

> *Never underestimate the effect*
> *of taking action on small things.*
> -Bruce Rhoades

You want your customer's experience to be delightful. Think one-stop shopping. Let no customer ask the same question twice. Your customer service goal is the seamless flow of communication. Patients need not repeat themselves. There's no need for duplication of activities. Insure that your customer's needs have been met to their satisfaction the first time.

"You hear it, you own it." No passing the problem from team member to team member. No excuses. "It wasn't my fault" or "It's not my job" must never be heard. See the customer's problem through to resolution and delight.

Cross-trained team members can do everything. Endless phone tag or explanations by countless team members is poor customer service. Answer all questions and resolve all situations immediately.

The desired feeling of each new and existing patient is, "I am important, and this is where I belong." In order to create this feeling, every team member, including the doctor, will need to be empowered to give immediate service recovery to the patient.

Review all of your patient touchpoints and actions during treatment. Give attention to taking care of the patient at every step of the dental service journey, and identify areas of potential improvement. Be sure that all team members are trained to take action on customer care needs at any time.

USE A MISSED APPOINTMENT TO CREATE A FAN

Patients miss appointments for a variety of reasons. Work calmly together towards rescheduling the missed appointment. Give your patients exactly the appointment time and day which they would like in whatever time frame you have available in your office.

Ask, "What time and day would you like to reschedule your appointment?" Reply, "I have a Wednesday at 5:00 p.m. available in nine weeks. Would you like that appointment or something sooner?" Offer to put your patient on a cancellation list for their desired appointment time sooner and offer to call your patient should you receive a cancellation.

Or, you could offer to have your patient wait that day of the missed appointment time to be accommodated into the present-day schedule. You and your team can use an overflow treatment chair to work the patient into the present schedule, or you can stay late to treat the patient that day and make your customer very happy.

All of these approaches work. It is your job as a customer service leader to get to the root of the problem of a missed appointment and create a solution. Accommodate your patients. After the appointment is over, re-evaluate the situation. With attention to customer service, your distraught patient will soon become a fan.

GREETING THE PATIENT

"Mr. Bond... Mr. James Bond?" Allow your patient to further introduce themselves and their family to you and your team. Use your patient's

COMMUNICATION

name immediately. "Welcome, James. We're so happy that you are here today."

Take time to read and memorize new patient's names. Post lists of new patient's names at the front desk computer station. Prepare to greet the new patient. Stand. Give the new patient and their family a warm welcome.

In our initial exam room, the treatment coordinator posts a welcome sign for the new patient in a clear plastic stand. It is visible to me, the doctor, during the new patient examination. In this way, you can easily look up and see the patient's name, and use it throughout the entire exam. Patients are moved by this personalized gesture. After the exam is completed, the sign is given to the new patient in their welcome folder. For a special touch, we have every team member and the doctor autograph the welcome sign. This will be their personal souvenir of their new patient experience.

SMALL TALK

Communication can be taught, learned, practiced, reviewed, and mastered. There are many forms, scripts, books, tapes, and courses that you and your office team can use to improve communication skills. Start with "How are you today?" and "What's new in your life?" If you are looking for a topic ask, "How are your kids?" People love to talk about themselves and their families.

Diffuse unpleasant topics or situations by injecting something new. Try, "Isn't it a beautiful day?" When the patient's appointment is over. Let the patient know that you enjoyed talking with them. Let them know that you look forward to talking with them again next time.

THE TEN MOST POWERFUL CUSTOMER SERVICE PHRASES

Eric Harvey, in his book *180 Ways to Walk the Customer Service Talk* prioritizes the ten most powerful customer service phrases according to the number of words. Life is short and I can't wait for dessert! Let's start with the most powerful word in customer service.

1. "YES."

Say "Yes."
-Wayne Dyer

AT YOUR SERVICE

If you remember nothing else from this entire book on customer service remember just one word: "Yes."

"Yes, we can do it! Yes, that time is available, Yes, Yes, YES!!!"

Joy is delivered when patients and their families get what they want. Focus on "Yes" actions with your customers and watch your practice grow.

Nothing is sweeter to a dentist's ears than hearing their excellent team saying "Yes" to patients. The next best thing is having the team say "Yes" to the dentist!

Many times, dentists are eager to say "Yes" to a patient and it is the team member who blocks the action of customer service by saying "No." Be aware of this in your dental office, take note, and eliminate this attitude. Turn nay-saying "No" employees into "Yes!" customer service team leaders.

The word "No" is the killer of customer service. Telling a customer what you "can't do" is a sure way to drive them away. When this happens, ask yourself, "Is it a can't do, or a won't do?" "Can't do" is perhaps lack of training or a systems problem which can be fixed. "Won't do" is a bad attitude.

Customer service is about doing, pleasing, accommodating, and making your customer happy. Customer service is about saying "YES!" YES is the most powerful word in the world of customer service and of life.

2. "Thank you."

If you only say one thing each day, "Thank you" is enough. To be recognized by "Thank you" warms the heart and makes one want to come back for more. Appreciation is one of the sweetest things in life.

Small "Thank you" gifts can also be used as symbols of appreciation. Reward tokens are a thank you. Gift cards are a thank you. A goody bag of oral health products or a Crest Oral B Hygiene Bundle is a thank you. Use the term "Thank you" generously.

3. "Glad you're here."

Without the customer, we would not have a dental practice. We would not have jobs in the service industry of dentistry. It's important to honor this statement by saying, "Glad you're here" to the patient.

It's also important to say, "Glad you're here" to each other. How well we treat each other is how well we will treat the customer. Let your team and patients know, "Glad you're here."

4. "How did we do?"

The late, great Mayor of New York, Ed Koch would ride the subway and stand on street corners asking, "How'm I doin'?" His great love was New York City and he wanted his city to be the best it could be.

The essence of a customer feedback program is the question, "How did we do?" Ask this question every day in either verbal or in written form and pay attention to the answers. Dental management consultant Joan Garbo encourages her clients to ask, "What could we do better?" and consider customer complaints as an opportunity for collaboration.

Be sure to address your customer complaint using the words "I respect," "I appreciate," "I admire," and "I agree" for smooth discussion of the constructive criticism. In relating to the customer, especially in the handling of complaints, these words are important for conveying empathy and letting your patient know that you hear them, that you understand them, and that you care.

Have your front desk person ask each patient, "How did we do?" This immediate customer feedback is the best (and most cost effective) customer service advice you will ever get.

5. "How may we SERVE you?"

Dentistry is a service industry. We are employed to serve. That is why the mission statement at Gorczyca Orthodontics has the word SERVE at its center.

Caring professionals SERVING valued patients.
-Gorczyca Orthodontics

The Ritz-Carlton, the premier service hotel in the country, has a simple service mission:

To be ladies and gentlemen, SERVING ladies and gentlemen.
-The Ritz-Carlton

Take a look at your mission statement. Does it have the word SERVICE or SERVING at its core?

6. "What is most convenient for YOU?"

It's not what is most convenient for US. It's "What is most convenient for YOU," the all-important patient. This is a powerful phrase. Of course, not every patient can be given every favorite appointment time. If so, every patient would probably come in at 7:00 p.m. after school, work, or dinner. Every dentist would be working a 24-hour shift and soon the dental professional would become a dental emergency room.

But this does exist. Dental offices in New York City are now offering extensive evening hours, running well into the night. Emergency dental clinics are being built and planned where doctors sleep over, on-call to answer emergency dental calls. As dentistry evolves, dental health providers will also be offering more options in terms of office hours.

Mark Olivieri, customer experience and key opinion leader manager at American Orthodontics, states that if you can be flexible, you can rule your dental market. Accommodations rule. If you can make appointment time work for the convenience of the patient, you are a winner.

In orthodontics, "after school at 5:00 p.m." is the most common "what is most convenient for you" response. Sometimes we must respond, "That appointment time is available in ten weeks. The doctor would like to see you in eight weeks. We have an appointment time in eight weeks at 3:00 p.m. Which would YOU prefer?" In this way, the patient can choose for themselves, "What is most convenient for YOU?"

7. "What else can I do for YOU?"

We never know what is on a patient's mind. It is possible to help the patient in many ways, such as by scheduling appointments, answering questions, and delivering messages to the doctor. Perhaps the patient needs reassurance. We want patients to leave our dental office happy, fulfilled, and eager to return.

Your patient has taken time to visit you. Take a minute to answer all of their questions by asking, "What else can I do for YOU today?"

8. "I'm not sure, but I will find out."

We are all problem solvers. The words, "That's not my job" should never be uttered in the dental office. This is what our patients pay us to do. You may not know the answer to your patient's question about insurance, but you can find out.

COMMUNICATION

Be a problem solver. Don't "pass the buck" by passing a question on to someone else. Take responsibility and control. Offer immediate customer service attention.

9. "Thank you for your business. See you again soon."

Each time a patient leaves your dental office, you never know, truly, if they will return again. Your parting words will be the words they carry with them in their memory for months to come. Make your parting words pleasant. Thank them for choosing your office. Encourage patients to return and refer others. Tell them how much you enjoyed seeing and speaking with them and let them know you are looking forward to seeing them again.

10. "I apologize for our mistake. Let me make it right."

Your patients don't expect you to be perfect. They do expect you to be honest. When something does not work out perfectly, admit it, apologize for it, correct it, and move on.

Nothing will go as far as showing your patients that you care. Make note of mistakes in your systems and implement corrections so these errors do not happen again. By eliminating blunders, your office will improve and move towards customer service excellence.

ELIMINATE NEGATIVE COMMUNICATION

I think you achieve a lot more through love than negativity.
-Alexa Chung

Imagine receiving this message:
"We REGRET to inform you that we CANNOT process your insurance payment since YOU have NEGLECTED to sufficiently provide US with your information. Complete this form and return it to us."

How does this make you feel? Now consider:
"We are so pleased to welcome you as a new patient to our dental family. Please allow me to handle all of your patient needs. It is my pleasure to assist you with the completion of your insurance information for prompt payment. Please call me, Veronica, anytime at (925) 757-

9000 at your earliest convenience. I am here to serve you in any way that I can."

Remove negative responses from your vocabulary. These would include phrases like, "We can't," "We never," and even "No problem." If a patient in line at the front desk hears negativity from a distance or just catches the negative word "problem," they may think that there are problems in your office which is incapable of excellent service delivery.

Avoid slang words such as "Huh," 'Yeah," "You guys," "Sure," and "Folks." The choice of polite verbal phrases makes your office more professional and gives your patients your highest respect.

Choose to focus always on positivity in your conversations and replies. Choose your words wisely. Use positive phrases like, "My pleasure," "I would be happy to," and "Yes, certainly." Avoid negativity like the plague.

Operational topics and management issues are of no concern to the patient. Talk about equipment service and repairs at private huddles. It is not the patient's concern if someone is absent from work that day. Protect your conversation when you are in front of patients "on-stage." "Off-stage" is where improvement conversations take place. Keep your office's "dirty laundry" to yourselves to be resolved behind closed doors.

HIPAA
Open discussion of patient treatment is a HIPPA violation. Discuss private diagnosis and treatment plan details with your patients in a designated treatment coordination area where others cannot overhear the conversation. Be cautious not to discuss one patient's procedure openly in front of another patient.

Photographic Communication
Remember, "A picture speaks a thousand words." For esthetic changes or treatment plan acceptance, use photographs whenever possible. Let intraoral photos to guide your conversation. Visually show the patient their proposed tooth changes. Have your patient indicate on the images, not only for clarification and accurate communication, but also for documentation of treatment plan acceptance and agreement. Use photography as a tool for dental communication.

Written Communication

The quality of your printed material reflects the quality of your office and your level of customer service. Forms of written communication in the dental office may include handwritten notes, formal letters, or practice newsletters. Personal notes are always special and a sign that you value your patient. Examples include thank you cards, Christmas cards, Thanksgiving cards, Birthday cards, or other friendly postcards. Take time to send a thoughtful and beautiful card as a communication gift of patient appreciation.

Printed Materials

Colors have power. Yellow is happy. Rainbows are fun. Red is attention getting and action producing. Blue is soothing. What color is your office brand? Choose a color which reflects your office culture and climate.

Your colors, font, and design represent your brand, your personality, and the quality of your dental treatment. Patients receive business cards, welcome folders, brochures, and invitations, all of which need updating for a contemporary look. Excellent educational materials are available from Krames Communication. Find them at www.Kramesstore.com. Create a resource area in your dental office and maintain a continuous supply. Be sure to label these products with your office name, telephone number, and logo. Make sure all brochures and instructions are flawless.

Communication Alignment

> *Always treat your employees exactly as you*
> *want them to treat your best customers.*
> -Stephen R. Covey

Studies have shown that when it comes to communication, thirteen times is the number of times employees need to hear something to absorb it. That means if you as the leader start today and review customer service goals and standards at every monthly team meeting this year, everyone will completely absorb your information and be aligned within just a little over a year from now.

Customer service goals need to be consistently reviewed. The Mission, Vision, Core Values, and Strategy need to be discussed again and again in your dental office. Communication goes in every direction from doctor to team, doctor to patient, team to doctor, team to patients, patients to team and doctor. To begin this process, the doctor is held accountable for communicating the responsibilities of outstanding customer service to the team. Having a communication protocol ensures that communication is aligned with the office's customer service priorities, whether they are specifically related to customer experience or some other initiative. It is important that everyone within the dental office be continually updated on the customer experience so that continual improvements can be made.

Chapter 5

ALIGNMENT

*Finding good players is easy.
Getting them to play as a team is another story.*
-Casey Stengel

Teamwork involves alignment in the creation of customer experience. Everyone on the team must be aligned, engaged, committed, and working together towards serving the patient. Here we replace the "I" of accountability with the "We" of alignment. Team alignment is essential for customer service systems to work. Implementation and maintenance of alignment systems is no easy task.

We all need to answer the "Why" of what we need to do for the patient. Why is working in dentistry purposeful to us? A dental office mantra can help to answer this question.

Your mantra solidifies alignment, determining who you hire, how you train your dental team, and the consistency of your management processes. Every team member must know the mantra, understand it, and deliver it. It needs to be firmly in place for alignment to work.

Your External Mantra

> *We will take great care of you.*
> -Richard J. O'Donnell, MD, UCSF

Mantras are active think. Mantras deliver an active process. They answer the questions, "How can I help this customer?" "How can I make their experience as effortless and joyful as possible?" A mantra keeps the team focused as well as aligned. "If I see it, I own it" becomes an individual service mantra for getting the customer service job done.

When I met my husband, an orthopedic oncologist at the UCSF Medical Center, he described his work as what he was put on earth to do—to help patients. All I could think was, "Wow! What dedication, conviction, and passion. His patients must love him." And they do!

The right mantra marks the beginning of alignment, teamwork, and your customer service journey. He taught me that his external mantra of, *"We will take great care of you"* is vital to his success. He may not have known that this was a mantra, but it is. I adopted it as mine as well. My husband and I both make it a habit to say this phrase to every patient before we leave the exam room. It is our sincere patient promise and it builds heartfelt trust. We believe that this represents customer service at its finest. It is the backbone of our teamwork and patient care.

Your Internal Mantra

> *We make you smile.*
> -Gorczyca Orthodontics

"We make you smile," summarizes many great benefits of dentistry: restoring dental health, giving someone a great smile, delivering happiness, having impactful relationships, and delivering outstanding customer service. It is a powerful internal mantra.

This mantra helps my team members understand our office's vision and mission. Get everyone on your team onboard with great mantras. Incorporate your mantras into smart hiring, training, service systems, and management, and you're sure to have consistent customer service alignment.

Use Your Mantra to Solve Problems

If you want something done, hire a busy mom.
                          -Kevin O'Leary

Mr. Wonderful from *Shark Tank* speaks the unfiltered truth when it comes to business decisions. One common thread he has found of high performing businesses is that they are led by women. He states that he has come to believe that if you want to find entrepreneurs who get things done, find busy moms who juggle millions of things, because somehow they manage to also run and grow a great business. One of his business mantras is, *"If you want something done, hire a busy mom."*

Putting your mantras into action with customers will help you maintain focus and resolve issues as they arise. Stating *"We will take great care of you"* will make your patient smile. To gain credibility and authority with the patients or parents you are trying to help begin by introducing yourself in an informative way. Sate your job title, years of service, and specialized training, and how long you have owned or managed the practice. Then state the facts:

- Whether their complaint had never happened before
- Apologize
- Repeat the complaint for understanding
- State how the problem will be solved
- Ask if they are now happy
- Thank them for their input

Players on your Team

With over twenty-seven years of experience of working in orthodontic practices as well as being a practice owner, I have found that there are two very hard jobs in the dental office—front desk patient coordinator, and "Office Manager." Let's explore both of these positions.

The Almighty Front Desk

Whether you call her the patient coordinator, receptionist, or concierge, the front desk person is the quarterback of your customer service. Your front desk is your front line of customer service delivery. This is the position which requires skill and personality to anticipate, listen, hear, process, and begin to resolve customer service issues. This team member must love people, have good judgment and reasoning skills, and be reliable.

The job of front desk concierge can be stressful. It will involve talking about patient finances. It may require that the customer service leader ask, in a pleasant and respectful manner, for payment of monies owed the dental office. It will involve discussing missed appointments, for which there may be a charge, and insurance non-payment. All of these topics must be discussed politely and discretely. Lastly, the front desk person herself must have excellent attendance to carry through on the important job which needs to be done.

Money is always a sensitive subject. Patients may get defensive when asked to pay an outstanding balance. Patients may even hang up the phone when asked for payment by the front desk customer service leader. The front desk patient coordinator will need to exhibit strength in determination, self-control, respect, and emotional intelligence. These talents grow with life experience. The front desk person must have the ability to relate to family situations with calmness and persistence. Such qualities of a great front desk patient coordinator are not easy to find, but once you find them in one such person, hold on to her for as long as you can.

Office Manager

Hospital quality scores are approximately 25% higher in physician-run hospitals than in manager-run hospitals.
-Stoller, Goodall & Baker

Years ago I was invited to a dental office manager's group meeting. I was sent by Patterson Dental to attend the national conference. I learned a lot from this experience, which I still carry with me today, which I feel will benefit you, my readers.

Doctors cannot join the dental office managers group. This group is only for dental office managers. Thinking that the group may be able to add something to my knowledge base, I returned to my office and asked who on my dental team might be interested in participating in this office managers group.

At first, my treatment coordinator agreed. So I put her in charge of our first "Office Managers" community meeting. This title of course brought prestige, as the words "office manager" were assigned to the person, who remained my treatment coordinator, whom I had hired and trained.

A few weeks later, the time came for the first meeting. Five minutes before starting, the newly minted "Office Manager" demanded a $6 per hour raise! She stated that she had received a job somewhere else for higher pay. I told her that we would miss her and I wished her well. There was no need for her to stay for the meeting. I would just run it myself.

Beware the title of "Office Manager" which, with or without added responsibilities, demands higher pay. The person holding this title position may deserve additional compensation, or they may not. This is only the first reason this title of "Office Manager" is problematic.

I decided that I would give this title of "Office Manager" a second try. At that time, I had an excellent records coordinator who also was in charge of my payroll. I asked her if she would like to participate in the office managers study group. At first she said she did not want to do it, but then she changed her mind.

What happened next is quite interesting. Although nothing had changed, suddenly this long-time records coordinator had no time to complete her downloading, cropping, and printing of the patient records, which she had done successfully as her job for several years. She fell behind in her regular work. When I asked about it, she stated that she did not have the time to complete her routine duties with "all the other things" that her new position of "Office Manager" required. What other things? Nothing had changed other than the figurative title of "Office Manager."

The perception was that things had changed. She was now a "manager." Communication with me, the doctor and practice owner, diminished. This team member suddenly started making decisions on her own, with which I, as the owner of the practice did not agree.

One new decision was to change payroll companies after twenty years of successful payroll service with our company. After two payrolls with the new online service, it became obvious that this new company offered no customer service. A human being was not assigned to our account. So, after two payrolls, we switched back to our original payroll company. This change led to a double payment of our quarterly payroll taxes in the amount of $18,000 overpayment to the IRS, which was electronically automatically paid when service for the new company was not successfully discontinued. I am still trying to resolve this matter with the IRS as I write this book.

Interaction with the other employees also became strained once the title of "Office Manager" was given. The "Office Manager" suddenly became critical of other team members who she had worked well with for years. The office became tense. Teamwork diminished.

My new "Office Manager" attended two national meetings and completed the fellowship process. After this was completed, we got a call from the national office managers study club telling us that we were "unofficial" until we paid $1,000 to join the office managers group. What had begun as a sincere interest in dental practice management had turned into a practice management, teamwork, and financial fiasco.

This second "Office Manager" team member also left our practice where she had worked successfully for fifteen years prior to becoming an "Office Manager." She is now an "Office Manager" somewhere else.

I am obviously not a fan of the title dental "Office Manager" for the dental office. For less than ten people, why couldn't the doctor be the leader of the team and management decision maker? Why would a liaison be needed when matters could be taken care of immediately by the doctor? Why complicate your office life? In a small office middle management only creates a layer of inefficiency for a job the doctor can do immediately him or herself. Giving a title certainly does nothing to improve teamwork or build a positive attitude work environment.

Imagine a basketball team where suddenly all the players are not equal, not a team, and one member starts to tell the other players what to do. It's a teamwork disaster. It can be the same for you in your dental office with an "Office Manager." Consider treating all of your team members equally, with fairness. Focus on individual performance and achievement. Assign management system jobs to each team member you already have in your practice. Have team members report their own achievements and progress at your monthly team meetings. Manager may not be a position you need in your dental practice. This function might best be reserved for the practice owner—the doctor.

Handling Complaints

> *Respect is earned.*
> *Honesty is appreciated.*
> *Trust is gained.*
> *Loyalty is returned.*
>   -Nishan Panwar

Problems in the dental office are inevitable. With problems come complaints. People are people. None of us are perfect and we all make mistakes.

"May I speak to the doctor?" These words reflect a break in customer service. Something or someone is out of line. Emergency lights start going off in the doctor's head like it's NASA calling to say, "Houston, we have a problem!"

Because the doctor is the owner of the practice and the authority, customers are generally more composed with the doctor than they are with the dental team members. I am often surprised when a team member puts me on the phone with a so-called "angry" patient and we calmly discuss a satisfactory solution to their problem with politeness and respect. The patient is usually very nice and satisfied. Yet, often as the doctor I was told that this same patient had just yelled at, berated, or hung-up on my front desk receptionist.

All dental office staff members need to think of themselves as frontline customer-facing service professionals. They need to have the authority to handle complaints and resolve them immediately at every touchpoint. Everyone needs to be continuously focused on service in order to help patients immediately solve their service problems. Each team member needs to be empowered to handle customer service inquiries and complaints, as they arise, without automatic escalation to the doctor. "May I speak to the doctor?" is something all dentists hope not to hear.

ALIGNMENT

I Love Getting to Know Patients and Being Part of a Team
Gwen, RDA, Orthodontic Assistant

"I first got into dental assisting through my friends who were dental assistants. They told me I would LOVE dental assisting! They were right. I do!

"I enjoy the fast pace of the orthodontic office. As an orthodontic assistant, I have my own chair, my own schedule, and ownership of the patient experience. As I seat my orthodontic patient and get them prepared to see Dr. Gorczyca, my patient and I have the opportunity for small talk and getting to know each other on a personal level. After two years of bi-monthly visits, we usually know each other very well. We have built a relationship. Getting to know the patient and their family is the best part of my job. Everyone on our team is very welcoming. We are aligned to give the best patient experience possible. Patient happiness is what our office is all about.

"I also enjoy being part of the outstanding team of customer service leaders at Gorczyca Orthodontics. Our team is very close. No one works alone or has an unfair work burden. We're a team working together. Every team member helps the others out. Clinical excellence, outstanding customer service, and a great patient experience are our personal and team goals. We stay focused and always put patient care first in our personal clinic decisions.

"Orthodontics is fascinating. We change lives. Our patients' smiles truly are our inspiration."

ALIGNMENT OF STRENGTHS

People who consistently apply "signature strengths" to their work experience less depression and more happiness on the job. To identify team member strengths, visit Values in Action Survey of Character Strengths at www.viacharacter.org. Developed by psychologists, it ranks twenty-four strong human qualities. This exercise will help place your team members in the right job and set up your customer service leaders for success.

To maximize your customer service leadership effectiveness, place team members into positions they love at which they excel. This will allow your team member to feel more joy in their work experience and to bask in what is already great about them.

Chapter 6

RESULTS

*Businesses are not successful because they earn a lot of money.
They earn a lot of money because they are successful,
and their success is a result of serving customers.*
-Frank Cooper

In his book, *The Customer Signs Your Paycheck*, author Frank Cooper describes results as "rewards given in The Law of Compensation." This law states that for every action there must be a reaction and that every act of service must be rewarded. In our free enterprise system or our economy, this reward is given in the form of money. In dentistry, we are successful not because we do a dental procedure. We are successful because we serve the customer.

Effective Customer Service Phrases
Take time to memorize these effective customer service responses to improve your service results. Positive phrases like these are the magic of customer service.

> "We are sorry that we caused you this problem."
> "I apologize for your inconvenience."
> "Please know that we take your concerns very seriously."
> "This is an oversight on our part."

"We will review this problem to make sure that this never happens again."
"How may I help you?"
"That's a good point; let me find out about this and how we can handle this for you."
"I'll be right with you."
"Let me finish. I will be happy to give you my total attention to help you."

Mediocre Customer Service Phrases

The words *I don't know* are killers of customer service. Customer service responses that do not address or resolve the problem include:

"We are sorry if we let this happen."
"We are sorry that this occurred."

without resolution. These responses do not make things right. Avoid happy talk. It is little better than remaining silent. Otherwise, you are delivering a mediocre customer service. Always express your intent to take corrective action.

Poor Customer Service Phrases

The poorest customer service responses do not take responsibility. They say things like:

"We are sorry IF we did something wrong."
"We are sorry that YOU feel this way."
"It is not our fault."
"I'm busy."
"You can take your business elsewhere."

Patients want timely responses to their customer service needs. Never argue with a patient. Whatever happened, chances are that in some way, it IS your fault. At Boys Town, a center giving boys an opportunity to turn their troubled lives around, Father Flannagan said, "There is no such thing as a bad boy." There is no such thing as a "bad patient," only practitioners not yet skilled in how to handle and care for all patients.

Management Systems

> *High expectations are the key to everything.*
> -Sam Walton

Systems matter. They produce effectiveness and efficiency and keep your practice running like a well-oiled machine. When systems are broken, it does not matter how friendly you are or how attractive you are, if you cannot fix your office problems, your customer will have a negative experience and may even leave your practice. Your management systems will need constant attention. We do not have leeway to make mistakes in dentistry. If you have an error, consider it a sign that you need to improve your systems and your customer service.

Surveys

> *Even your most loyal customers always have a choice about where to take their business.*
> -Marilyn Suttle

How are you going to find and handle lost customers? Follow-up. If you have lost a customer, send a survey and find out why. Thank your patients for their years of business. It is only by getting this information in the form of customer feedback that you will be able to improve. It may be one sub-par employee. You don't want to lose more customers for the same reason that remains unknown to you. Your patients' opinions of your practice matter.

    I remember it like it was yesterday. The destruction of a notable firm brought about by the addition of one new employee. The firm had many years of a reputation of excellence and customer care. Then a new partner was taken onboard. Suddenly the professionalism sank. Bad language started being used and even posted on the Internet. Client confidentiality was lost. Customers began being treated with disrespect. Yet, the company was clueless. In the end, the founding partners and new partner entered into a lawsuit against each other. In the meantime, the customers left.

If by chance you hired a "bad apple," you need to know right away in order to make a timely change. A customer service survey is one way to collect and document the data you need to have to make necessary changes.

Three Questions to Ask Your Least Happy Customers

1. What are we missing?
2. What could we do differently?
3. If you could have a magic wand, what would you like to see here?

Results matter. There is only one way to find out what your customers want: ask them. Track your results through your own customer service survey. Keep score. Your customer satisfaction survey is the tool by which you can achieve your goals for outstanding results.

Compliments

*People are happier when they focus on the positive,
yet companies rarely give them that chance.*
-Sterling Bone

Beginning your customer survey with what researchers call an "open-ended positive solicitation" yields positive results. A question like, "What went well during your treatment with us?" will help restore patient memories of well-being. A "share a compliment" program will build appreciation between customer and employees. Asking for positive responses shifts the customer focus from "land mines" to "gold mines." Find out what your patients love and do more of that.

Studies have shown that asking for a compliment can raise Net Promoter Scores (a common loyalty metric) by as much as 15% and boost purchase intentions by as much as 25%. Let your patients know that "you strive for five." Continue on with the standard question, "What can we do better?" to improve service trends and keep your customers happy at the same time.

Complaints

It is only by friction that we polish.
-Mary Parker Follett

Take the stigma out of complaints. Don't get stuck in thinking that you never want to receive feedback. Your toughest critics are your greatest source of information and often end up being your biggest cheerleaders. Listen to the people who tell you what you need to hear. Initially, it may not be what you want to hear, and it may make you feel uncomfortable, but you can turn this feedback into a very positive experience and benefit for your office.

Ask daily for customer service feedback. "What could we do better?" Never argue with a customer. If you receive a complaint, it is possible to say, "You're absolutely right," "I totally agree!" Focus on the resolution of the problem and put aside your hurt feelings or disappointment. Don't take constructive criticism personally. Improve your systems and stay focused on the patient and your customer service goals.

Seven Steps to Handling a Customer Service Complaint

Your most unhappy customers are your greatest source of learning.
-Bill Gates

Here it comes. Take a deep breath. Maintain control at all times. As you handle a complaint, here is a seven-step process you can use.

1. Listen
2. Ask questions
3. Propose a solution
4. Ask if the solution is satisfactory
5. Ask what would be satisfactory to the customer
6. Grant another solution
7. Explain why this solution would satisfy them

If you make a mistake, admit it, apologize for it, fix it, and move on.

Don't get defensive. Customers really don't expect you to be perfect. Don't "pass the buck" to another team member or make excuses. Make it an office policy to accept, "If I see it, I own it." Follow that by, "I resolve it." Make it right. Make a service recovery. Fix whatever needs to be fixed for your customer.

Three Parts of a Customer Service Apology

Rule #1- The customer is always right.
Rule #2- If the customer is ever wrong, re-read Rule #1.
-Stew Leonard

Customers expect sincere commiseration for their inconvenience. Listening is perhaps the most important ingredient of customer service. Empathizing is one sure way to lighten the burden of patient complaints.

There are three factors to consider when apologizing:

1. The truth of what happened with an apology,
2. A remedy to ease the pain and make things right, and
3. An ear to listen to the customer and respect their feelings.

The customer may not always be right. Service may not always run smoothly. No matter the situation, the customer will always be your highest priority. Your sights should be set on pleasing the customer.

Consider sincere complaints as a gift. They give you and your dental team the opportunity to make things right. You may not be able to make every patient happy all of the time, but you can try. To be best able to do this without driving yourself crazy, it's important to understand the four types of complainers.

Four Types of Complainers

In his book, *The Customer Signs Your Paycheck,* Frank Cooper describes the relative point of view that sets the tone of the relationship between you and your customer as "OK-ness." He describes four basic positions of the patient-office relationship:

1. I'm OK-You're OK
2. I'm Not OK-You're OK
3. I'm OK-You're Not OK
4. I'm Not OK-You're Not OK

Let's look at these four situations next as they apply to your dental office.

1. I'M OK-YOU'RE OK: A HEALTHY RELATIONSHIP.

A healthy patient relationship is what most patients exhibit in our dental offices. People who accept this life position recognize their own self-worth. They see people as being very much like themselves. They have respect for themselves and others. Their complaints and suggestions are a pleasure to receive and it is easy to work with patients who are OK, who are a delight. They don't get upset over small matters. They understand that no one is perfect. They are fair.

OK employees are valuable assets to their doctor and their patients. These employees are service-oriented and give customers the kind of attention they deserve. This positive and healthy self-image team member is critical for the success of your dental office. Positivity does more to ensure the success of your dental office than virtually any other asset. It is therefore critical to have positive team members in a positive frame of mind who know they are "OK."

2. I'M NOT OK-YOU'RE OK: A JUVENILE RELATIONSHIP.

Early in life, we gauge our personal success on the smiles or frowns of other people. Some people, even as adults, never escape this juvenile feeling of inferiority. Some people even as adults base their own inner self-image on the reactions of other people. If people are smiling, they're OK. If people are frowning, they're not OK. These people believe that they must shape their behavior to gain acceptance. They may advertise their inferiority. They have an inferiority complex.

We must go out of our way to make "I'm Not OK" patients feel good about themselves. We accomplish this effect by complimenting them with sincere comments and by demonstrating care and respect. Because these people seek the approval of others, they will return to places of business where they feel OK. Go out of your way to make them feel valued.

3. I'M OK-YOU'RE NOT OK: A CYNICAL RELATIONSHIP.

Cynics don't like themselves and they don't like you, either. Cynics don't like anyone! They complain every time they speak. They seldom trust people with whom they are doing business and you're no exception.

"I'm OK-You're Not OK" customers are difficult. With cynics, it is important to accentuate the positive and not let them affect your good feelings about yourself and your dental office. There is very little you can do to change these people's attitudes except provide them with excellent customer service that is prompt and courteous. Maybe you'll get them to smile. Don't give up. Maybe you'll even get them to say "You're OK."

4. I'M NOT OK-YOU'RE NOT OK: AN ANTI-SOCIAL NARCISSISTIC RELATIONSHIP.

"I'm Not OK-You're Not OK" patients are the most difficult of all to treat. They believe that they are always right. You may be always wrong in the minds of this patient. If there is a disagreement, they will act as if there is no question about their correctness. They may even question your treatment itself, declaring they know more about dentistry than the dentist!

The "I'm Not OK-You're Not OK" personality type is a selfish personality. They have little respect for other people. They are nice to you as long as there is a direct pay-off to them. This personality type needs excellent customer service and special favors that others do not receive.

The "I'm Not OK-You're Not OK" patient has few friends. They have little opportunity to experience the joy of loving relationships. They may have even come from an abusive family.

At worst, "I'm Not OK-You're Not OK" persons could approach a criminal mindset. They have little regard or empathy for others. They don't care if they make your life miserable. They are 100 percent out for themselves.

These patients jump from dentist to dentist. They may even go for five consultations before choosing a dental specialist. They may go through five dentists during a three-year period when seeking veneers. One diagnostic wax-up is not enough for them. They need two or even three, and still may not start treatment in your office.

It is not easy to handle the "I'm Not OK-You're Not OK" patient. If you can overlook their dysfunction and care for them, you will be rewarded with the satisfaction of helping this person add joy to their life. With the "I'm Not OK-You're Not OK" patient you have two choices: treat this patient with understanding, kindness, and compassion, and make the world a better place, or dismiss them as patients.

The "I'm Not OK-You're Not OK" patient creates two major problems in the dental office. First, they don't follow directions because they think they know more than the dental health professional. Second, they waste valuable time in your office while creating aggravation. I don't wish an "I'm Not OK-You're Not OK" patient on anyone.

Proceed with caution and document all transactions with writing and photographs. Our fight or flight instinct tells us to run. They are, however, human beings who need our help.

Impossible Patients

There is a point at which a perturbed, displeased, disappointed, or angry complainer becomes a crazy. In his book, *Hug Your Haters*, author Jay Baer describes crazies as "customers who cannot be satisfied or mollified, regardless of how and when you interact with them." Such customers can be frightening or downright dangerous. There are three ways of dealing with unhinged customers: ignore them, research them, or hug them.

You may want to have a rule of "We don't do crazy" or "We treat teeth not feelings." Ninety-nine point nine percent of your patients are kind and level-headed. Once a person crosses the threshold of crazy, you may want to document their every word and communicate with them in writing, supplemented with clinical photos. If they need to communicate, ask them to e-mail you and tell them that you will reply by e-mail. Archive everything going forward.

You can also "research" an unreasonable patient. You can start by making inquiries of the patient herself. Are they having any problems in life? You might reach out to family members, enlisting support. Other dentists on the multidisciplinary team can also provide insight. The complainer can still be acknowledged and given empathy. The more upset the customer is, the more opportunity you have to calm them down and turn them around. Take time to understand your customers.

Service Recovery

To be of real service, one must be willing to constantly discover exactly what the customer wants or needs—and then provide it.
-Mark Ursino

No matter what happens with a patient, always be polite and maintain a calm demeanor. Never argue because even if you win, you lose. Each person is valuable. Be sure not to treat anyone as if they were a liar or a cheat. This is never the appropriate response, and even unexpressed feelings of such will not help your cause. Most people are honest and fair. It is unfair of dental professionals to penalize all good patients because a small minority are dishonest, or do not make payments.

At first, an unhappy customer may make you feel anxious. Take a deep breath, calm down, and emotionally embrace the critic. They are your greatest source of learning. They will help your dental office to improve.

Customers know and understand that service can occasionally go wrong. Most people are reasonable. Service recovery is imperative. It is always appreciated. Whatever the problem is, identify it, isolate it, and then fix it. Most problems are easiest to resolve in the early stage. The longer the customer waits for a service resolution, the more frustrated they get.

Everyone on your team needs to understand the importance of honesty in immediate service recovery. A total customer service disaster is to ignore or hide mistakes. In my book *Beyond the Morning Huddle,* I emphasize the teamwork philosophy of Duke men's basketball coach Mike Krzyzewski, Coach K, that "Only the truth shall be spoken." Whether things are good or bad, everyone on the team needs to know about it right away. Knowing the truth allows corrections to be made so as to improve customer service.

There is no "Fake it till you make it," when it comes to healthcare. The truth of the situation must always be presented without criticism so that corrective action can be taken to achieve results. Team members must feel comfortable asking for help and other team members must feel comfortable giving help. If need be, hire an outside consultant to help you gain order. This will avoid future surprises of items unattended should a team member leave their job.

Tracking Customer Results

When leadership is alive in the dental office, everyone serves with passion and is engaged in making the customer experience their top priority. Everyone on the dental team individually is responsible for how they treat their patient and how they deliver outstanding customer service. Surveys will have individual team members' names for comment. Everyone is a leader and plays a key role in building a customer service culture.

Tracking customer service results will never end. Make note of things mentioned in your surveys. Keep track. Keep improving. Check your systems. Call your own phone. Is it answered within the first three rings? Is it answered with a smile? How does your team look? Every day, take a moment to walk around and observe how every member of your team is treating customers. Ask your patient, "How were things today?"

The Annual Customer Service Award

Every act of service must be rewarded.
-Frank Cooper

Highlighting performance puts customer service goals at the forefront. Actions which are rewarded get repeated. In a culture of excellence, the annual Customer Service Award is the highest form of recognition and achievement. This award can be highlighted at your annual team offsite and discussed at your monthly team meeting. Annual winners can be listed in the Team Handbook. You could even have a plaque in your office citing the winners each year. Take time to appreciate an outstanding individual for a job well done. They serve as a role model for other Customer Service Award winners of the future.

Chapter 7

EXCELLENCE

*Excellence isn't about working extra hard to do what you're told.
It's about taking the initiative to do work you decide is worth doing.*
-Seth Godin

In his book *Poke the Box*, Seth Godin reminds us that excellence is a personal, passionate way to do your job. It's a calling. It is perhaps the reason you were put on this earth. Excellence takes initiative. It's a personal urgency to change lives through your work of dentistry.

World-class excellence requires quality through action. Excellence at anything in life requires discipline. It is through the passionate engagement of customer service leaders within the dental office that an office achieves patient care excellence.

BE EXCELLENT AT HELPFUL

Customer service industry leader Zappos doesn't leave anything to chance when it comes to orientation of customer service leaders. Zappos emphasizes a commonality of how employees go through their days delivering happiness to their customers. Great experiences are delivered by passionate people. Here is the Zen of Zappos.

EXCELLENCE

Ten Principles of Conduct from Zappos

1. Deliver Wow through Service
2. Embrace and Drive Change
3. Create Fun and a Little Weirdness
4. Be Adventurous, Creative, Open-Minded
5. Pursue Growth and Learning
6. Build Open and Honest Relationships through Communication
7. Build a Positive Team, Family Spirit
8. Do More with Less
9. Be Passionate and Determined
10. Be Humble

According to Zappos CEO Tony Hsieh, the key to success is focusing on the happiness of those around you—your customers and your employees. Hsieh knows that not every employee will be a cultural fit, passionate about the work they were hired to do, or happy to serve customers. Once Hsieh discovers those who do not fit the company culture, in terms of being burned out, negative or unwilling of living the core values, he offers a graceful exit by providing $2,000 compensation for their time upon their voluntary leave-taking. In this way, he effectively encourages unengaged employees to move on.

It's a great idea to offer an employee not suited for your office culture $2,000 to move on. If the employee stays, they will end up costing your business more. Should you ever hear the words "I think I'll quit," or "I feel like quitting," state that you are happy to accept this dispassionate person's resignation and give them a severance package. Don't prolong the inevitable. Unenthused employees will leave sooner or later. In the meantime, they will reduce your customer service brand and make those around them miserable. Follow Tony Hsieh's lead: encourage people who do not fit the soul of your dental office to leave.

Office Reward System

We are what we repeatedly do.
Excellence therefore, is not an act, but a habit.
-Aristotle

You get what you reward. Your employee rewards programs must focus on service. For improvements and excellence in customer service, work on strengths, highlight strengths, and reward strengths. Little by little, your team of customer service leaders will improve as things fall into place.

Review customer service achievements in an effort to improve and maintain what you have worked hard to establish. Discuss what customer service excellence means to each team member. Try to repeat customer service actions which have been deemed worthy by your patients. Emulate customer service excellence which you have enjoyed at other businesses.

Keep a customer service excellence notebook. Save patient responses and reviews that thank you and highlight your excellence in patient care.

Team Excellence

Excellence is achieved by a culture of continuous learning and improvement. Your customer service leaders will rarely rise above the level of performance and expectation that you have set for them. Perfection is impossible to achieve. But be honest with your team about the level of excellence for which you are aiming, and what needs to be improved to achieve it. If your team thinks that everything is acceptable or excellent, what incentive do they have to improve?

Joseph A. Michelli, in his book *The New Gold Standard,* outlines actions which have helped the Ritz-Carlton achieve customer service success. By entrusting the "Ladies and Gentlemen" service leaders of the Ritz-Carlton to offer individualized service, the customer experience is mastered and enriched. This same philosophy can be applied to your dental office. Here are some organized action items which will improve your team customer service excellence.

Thirteen Action Items for Team Excellence

1. Avoid the "I'll take anyone" syndrome when understaffed or hiring.
2. Involve current team members in the interview process of the new hire.
3. Offer an extensive new employee orientation process lasting up to ninety days.
4. Require and pay new employees to read the Team Handbook prior to the first day of work.
5. Use orientation to review your core values, mission, vision, and mantras.
6. Educate and develop team members to make them customer service leaders.
7. Conduct a monthly team meeting to review office results.
8. Discuss survey feedback about breakdowns in management systems and correct them.
9. Allow employees to suggest improvements needed for your office.
10. Celebrate accomplishments of individual team members, your office, and your team.
11. Celebrate tenure anniversaries.
12. Reward customer service excellence monthly, annually, and publicly.
13. Give an annual customer service award to the most outstanding service team member.

Ask at your monthly team meetings, "What three things could we improve this month?" and, "What goals have we achieved this past month that we set for improvement at our last team meeting?" Set improvement goals and come up with an action plan. Review your results and move on to your next office improvement project. A set plan for steady and continuous improvement will give your dental office a high customer service rating on the excellence meter.

A Culture of Excellence

You'll never have a product of price advantage again.
They can be easily duplicated,
but a strong customer service culture can't be copied.
    -Jerry Fritz

We can all work towards creating the ultimate dental patient experience. The opportunity is there for all of us to achieve. But if we don't try every day to be better than we were the day before, we will never achieve the nirvana of excellence. This constant quest is what drives your patient experience and delights everyone who comes into contact with your dental office and its people. When we strive for excellence, everyone is transformed along the way.

Excellence is Hard to Achieve
Dr. Ann Marie Gorczyca, Orthodontist
Founder of Gorczyca Orthodontics

"Whether it be clinical excellence, customer service excellence, or the excellence of the patient experience, the pursuit of excellence is what gets me out of bed in the morning. It makes me write books, read, study, and try to improve.

"There are many levels of excellence in the dental profession. In orthodontics, we have clinical excellence represented by the American Board of Orthodontics. The feedback process is invaluable in raising clinical acumen. Orthodontists also have the Angle Society, which is devoted to excellence in orthodontic treatment. General dentists may become Fellows of the Academy of General Dentistry, the American Academy of Cosmetic Dentistry, the Spear Institute, the Pankey Institute, or the Seattle Study Club. Continued study and self-evaluation of case results improve clinical excellence.

"Excellence in customer service is recorded by our patient care surveys. We review what is written and either do more of what is found to be excellent or improve areas which are lacking.

"A great patient experience is ultimately rewarded by the referral of more new patients. This is our greatest reward for customer service excellence.

"I am humbled by knowing that there is so much more we can all do as dentists, business owners, employers, and customer service leaders. I feel blessed that in my lifetime, I have had the opportunity to try my best at Gorczyca Orthodontics."

Part II

CARE

*The secret of caring for your patients
is in caring for your patients.*
-Francis Peabody, MD

C ustomers are special people. They have feelings, personalities, and names. My orthodontic patients and their families are important to me. The language people use when referring to their customers actually signals how they see themselves relating to them.

Do you call your customer a new exam, a start, a patient, a recall, or a case? Or, do you refer to them by name? How do you consider your customers? Do you treat them similar to shoppers walking into a jewelry store? Are they there to check out what you have to offer? If so, will you treat them as such? Or, will you treat them as a valued human being?

A dental office's most vital asset is its patients. They are your boss. Without new patients, the dental office would soon be out of business. When you continue to satisfy and over-deliver to your customers, not only do they continue to do business with you, but they enthusiastically recommend you to their family and friends. This is the lifeline of your dental practice.

Chapter 8

FRIENDLINESS

Every business is built on friendship.
-J. C. Penney

Friendliness is the most fundamental of customer needs. Take time to be friends with your patients. The more you know and care about your patients, the better that experience will be.

Can friendliness be created? Making a new friend simply starts with saying "Hi!" This is how friendliness is perceived. Have a special program of preparation for greeting the new patient the first time they enter your office.

Friendliness never fails. Hire for friendliness, train for knowledge. You can't train "nice." You can't teach someone to be happy, friendly, or to care. You need to hire a person already smiling who loves people, enjoys friendship, and is honored to serve others. You never get a second chance to make a good first impression.

People do business with people they like. In order to gain new patients, you and your team must be likeable. In order to be likeable, you must first like your patients and be friendly. To like your patient, get to know them, individually, as a person. Once you have done this, it will show that you authentically care. You are taking the time necessary to build a relationship.

The Patient Experience

> *Making customers evangelists is about*
> *creating experiences worth talking about.*
> -Valeria Maltoni

A customer service tune-up will yield a positive return on investment. In 2012, a poll published in *TIME*, commissioned by Parature, a customer service software company, reported that poor customer service costs US companies $80 billion in lost sales per year for an average of sixty percent of potential business. That's a forty percent conversion rate by US companies! This surprising fact may make you think, *Wow! I better focus on not losing customers.* Or, it may make you think, *Great! With excellent customer service there's a lot of business out there for the taking.* With statistics like these, don't leave your customer service patient experience to chance!

Put a smile on your face, be happy, and be grateful. Sounds easy, but for some it is not. Friendliness is reflected by actions and attitudes. Friendliness is a mirror—you get what you give. The single most common word in the rating of outstanding customer service is "friendly." Friendliness is perhaps the most important attribute for outstanding customer service.

In order for your patients to feel your dedication to their customer service, they must first feel your friendliness, warmth, and caring disposition. This is reflected first by being happy to see your patient and taking time to talk with them. This can be especially important in the face of a busy schedule. Don't forget to give individual attention and the personal touch in every situation, even when being understaffed, or in a moment of frustration.

By delivering a friendly experience consistently, your dental practice will be taken out of the commodity-driven price-sensitive corner of the dental industry and placed center stage in the lime light of five-star service excellence. By giving your patients something extra-special, going above and beyond expectations, your patient experience will not only be memorable, it can also be amazing.

FIFTEEN PATIENT-FRIENDLY EXPERIENCES

A smile is the universal welcome.
-Max Eastman

1. WELCOME QUESTIONNAIRE

If you don't know the patient's name, you can start the interaction by saying, "Hi, I'm so-and-so. Welcome to XYZ dental office." The patient will most likely tell you their name in reply. Use the new patient's name early on. Having a printed sign at the front desk to welcome the new patient by name will help you to remember their name.

Use the patient's name throughout their appointment and try to say their name at least three times. Use "Mr." or "Mrs." or "Ms." as appropriate. Use a title unless you have their permission to call them by a preferred first name or nickname.

People like to have their name pronounced correctly. I have spent my entire life stating, "It's Gorczyca, like the island of Cor-si-ca." Make notations in your patient files of the phonetic spelling of the patient's name with a possible way to remember it. Next time you or a team member comes in contact with the patient, you will know the correct way to say their name.

2. FRIENDS OF BUSINESS LIST

Peter Shankman, in his book, *Zombie Loyalists,* describes the most outstanding and loyal customers as Friends of Business (FOB) Zombies. These are your practice ambassadors. They love your business and they are happy to be part of it. These are the remarkable people who feed your practice and make your day fun. They refer family and friends.

They make each day fun, those FOBs (Friends of Business). If your office is fun and friendly, you will have achieved the first and second rules of outstanding customer service. These are the special people who care about your business. They will give you honest feedback. To get honest feedback that can improve your customer service, have a patient survey. Ask your patients, "What can we do better?" Then do it!

Make a list of your top ten patients and do something special for them right now. Send them a card or like them on Facebook. Tell them you're thinking of them, and you can't wait to see them again next time.

FRIENDLINESS

Let's look at what you could do to create an amazing patient experience for all of your patients. You want all of your patients to be FOBs. Here are a few suggestions.

Have each team member say "Hi" or "Hello" to every patient by name.
Ask about the patient's family.
Shake your patient's hand.
Do a fist bump.
Give a high-five.
Include your patients in fun activities.
Talk to your patients about their passions.
Tell your patients how much you appreciate them.
Make your patients part of your office family.
Tell your patient you love having them as a patient.
Treat your patient like a VIP.
Thank your patient for choosing your office.
Give your patient a thank you gift or card.
Tell your patient you can't wait to see them again at their next appointment.

3. SURPRISES

*Surprise is the greatest gift
which life can grant us.*
-Boris Pasternak

It was just another school party. Then I saw it. The amazing three-tiered chocolate fountain on the center Valentine's Day table. This crown jewel of centerpieces transformed eating strawberries, pineapple, and grapes into a party adventure. It was simply incredible.

You can also give out single roses on Valentine's Day or have an edible treat. Whatever holiday or theme you choose, making a day special will be fun, memorable, and remarkable for both your patients, and the entire office team.

A small surprise is a gift. It doesn't have to be much; it could even be your time. It could be a special greeting or phrase or farewell. Whatever your surprise, make each dental appointment fun and memorable, every time.

You may want to give your customers an experience in the form of an invitation to a party or a contest. You may want to touch their senses by giving them a poem or a book. Whatever it is, once given or once done, your patient will be looking forward to their next appointment.

Tokens of office swag, something with your office name on it, fun and colorful, can also be a great surprise. A mug, pen, T-shirt, or baseball cap makes your patient feel like part of your office team or family. Whatever it is, your patients will use it or wear it often, and tell others about your thoughtfulness. This is the biggest benefit of great customer service—internal marketing.

Is your office colorful? If not, add a little color. Whether in the form of decorations, flowers, or uniforms, color stimulates the senses. There's a rainbow of possibilities. Stimulate the eyes and imagination to produce a great patient experience.

4. FLAVORED GLOVES

Years later, one of our long-time patients gave us a five-star review on Yelp and wrote that her favorite thing about our office was the flavored gloves! Always a conversation piece as well as a fashion statement, flavored gloves give the dental "hands-in-the-mouth" experience a bit of excitement.

Available in multiple colors and with fruit or bubble gum flavors, these apparel items will not only delight patients, but give your office excellent "word-of-mouth" marketing. The colors and flavors of these gloves change throughout the year. You will soon hear, "What's that great smell?" or "Smells like strawberry." Patients simply love flavored gloves!

5. HYGIENE KITS AND GOODY BAGS

Give your patients the gift of oral health. Whether you give a hygiene bundle from Crest Oral B, or a single new toothbrush, hygiene updates are something patients look forward to at every dental appointment.

Oral hygiene bundles come prepackaged with an Oral B toothbrush, oral rinse, toothpaste, and floss, giving your patient all that they need for ideal oral health. Kids' packs come with a cute backpack. Children love them and moms are excited to create enthusiasm about brushing.

Goody bags with toothbrushes, floss, and paste are always convenient as in-office gifts or as school or special program giveaways. Giving the goody bag toothbrushes is a great reminder for your patients to throw the old toothbrush away.

FRIENDLINESS

6. OFFICE T-SHIRTS

Is your office T-shirt worthy? Make your patients feel like they're part of your team by giving them their own office T-shirt. Once the patient wears their shirt to their appointment as a member of your club, give them a small reward. It is a great feeling to look out into your reception room and see your happy, smiling patients all wearing their office T-shirts like members of your family or cheerleaders on your dental team.

7. TOOTH WHITENING GIFTS

There are many opportunities to give a gift to a special patient. Maybe someone will be in a beauty pageant and could use a tooth whitening kit. Maybe you discover that the patient is passionate about a hobby, and you send them an appropriate magazine subscription. Knowing your patients well and sharing their joy can be some of life's magical moments. Take time to be thoughtful, and your patients will be thoughtful in return.

8. AWARD TOKENS

Kids love rewards. Consider giving a reward token for good oral hygiene, good orthodontic appliance maintenance, or good behavior during an appointment. Redeem tokens for prizes and watch the fun start. Whether, a physical prize or gift card, the reward process is fun, and gives kids and adults alike something to anticipate during their appointment.

9. A PATIENT APPRECIATION PARTY

> *Appreciation is a wonderful thing:*
> *It makes what is excellent in others*
> *belong to us as well.*
> 									-Voltaire

Small business groups encourage consumers to "Shop local," or to "Buy local." As a dentist, you should "Do local" well. When you take care of the community, good things happen. Be kind. Thank your loyal customers for choosing your dental office.

One great way you can show your appreciation to your customers and to your community is to hold a Patient Appreciation Party. Whether at a water park, roller rink, bowling alley, museum, or ice cream fair in the office parking lot, an Appreciation Party is often a patient highlight of the year. Your generosity will be admired and discussed. Your community outreach will enable you to meet more people. Your event will surely create a local community buzz.

10. CONTESTS AND GIVEAWAYS

To stay fresh, interesting, remarkable, and exciting, your office will need to be in a state of constant change and imagination. Give everyone something to look forward to at their next visit. Keep your customer service momentum and engagement moving forward.

Contests are one way to engage patients in a fun office experience. Once integrated into your office, a contest can motivate patients to want to return to their next visit with the anticipation of a new event. This effort need not be expensive. As an example, you can run a contest to guess the number of Lego pieces in a Mason jar. Or, you can have a coloring contest centered around a holiday theme or sports event. And, coloring isn't just for kids anymore! Adults have caught on to the coloring fad, which can also add a colorful element of relaxation to waiting room stays!

I like giveaways that are for everyone, where everyone is a winner. Whether it is a pen, pencil, T-shirt, or a sports bottle, gifts with your insignia are a customer service marketing win-win.

11. COMPLETION CELEBRATION

Getting your braces off, an implant placed, or veneers completed is a special event. You've waited for many months, maintained your oral hygiene, not eaten hard candy, and attended many appointments. Celebrate Debond Day with your patient by giving them a special gift. Sing them a song. Roll out the red carpet. Make them feel like a VIP.

Forty years later, I can still remember the event of my personal Debond Day. It is the only day I remember my dad taking off of work. I was so proud to show my parents my new smile. It was a very special day indeed! Celebrate this special day with your patients. Perhaps every patient feels this way when they are done with a long dental procedure.

12. BEFORE AND AFTER PHOTOS

The transformation of a patient's smile translates to their personality and their life. Capture it with before and after photos. This montage is a constant reminder of the improvement your patient has made by undergoing dental treatment. Smiles change lives. Let your patient see their improvement in oral health, which contributes to their happy and healthy life.

I always tell my patients, "Put this before and after photo on your fireplace mantle for all the world to see." Patients think I am kidding, but I'm not!

13. SPECIAL CARDS

Greeting cards are a nice gesture of appreciation. Thanksgiving cards are always my personal favorite because they give us the opportunity to say, "Thank you." We send these not only to our patients but to our referring offices.

Holiday cards are an opportunity to enclose a picture of your customer service team with their names while sending good wishes. Birthday cards are a special treat. Send a thoughtful note whenever possible. Handwritten notes are a rare gesture of appreciation.

14. CARE CALLS

> *Do the right thing,*
> *do the best you can,*
> *and always show people you care.*
> -Lou Holtz

Care calls by the doctor after a long or difficult procedure are always appreciated. In my own dental community, the oral surgeons are the masters of post-care calls. They call every patient of the day post-surgery to check how they are doing. This not only shows the patient that you care about the recovery process, but most likely reduces additional calls later that evening.

As an orthodontist, I often call patients who have come in for an initial exam to ask if they have any additional questions. I am amazed how many patients I personally end up scheduling to start their orthodontic treatment.

Call patients who have been missing and have not come in for a while to inquire how they are doing. Perhaps they are having a personal difficulty, which is important for you to know. This information will help you understand and accommodate the patient even better in the future.

15. THE DENTAL SPA EXPERIENCE

I love my own dentist and his hygienist. I think of the office of Dr. Ken Dupree of Antioch, California, as a spa experience. My hygienist, Wendy, is extremely gentle and kind. She covers me with a warm blanket slightly heated in the dryer. During my dental hygiene appointment, she does not talk much so that I can relax. Smooth jazz is playing in the background and a scented candle is burning in the hallway, spreading a beautiful fragrance into the treatment room. As a busy wife, mother, and orthodontist, this is one of my favorite times to relax.

Dr. Dupree is an extremely gentle dentist. That's why I chose him. When he gives an injection, I can barely feel it. He is meticulous in all of his procedures and this is also reflected by the cleanliness of his office, which is impeccable. He does first-class work, and he is committed to excellence. It is a privilege to be his patient.

After my dental cleaning and exam are over, my hygienist hands me a warm towel, which she has heated in the microwave, to wipe my face. On the way out, I have a pleasant conversation with the ladies at the front desk. They ask about my family. Dana, the doctor's wife, makes my next appointment. They offer me a stick of my favorite sugar-free gum and hand me my hygiene goodie-bag. The overall dental experience could not be any better. I look forward to every time I go back!

Friendly people are just plain good to be around. Some people are friendlier than others but like any other skill, friendliness can be developed for you and your team in your dental office. All it takes is self-awareness and practice. There is tremendous potential in increasing your friendliness quotient and even the smallest good deed.

A random act of kindness can help you and your practice become wealthier, healthier, happier, and wiser. This is the power of nice. Medical malpractice lawyer Alice Burklin states, "I've never had a potential client walk in and say, 'I really like this doctor and I feel terrible about doing it, but I want to sue him.' People just don't sue doctors they like." Medical research Wendy Levinson observed shows physicians never sued versus those who had been to court at least twice. Those never sued spoke to their patients for an average of three minutes longer than the ones with litigious patients. They had softer voices and used humor more.

So take some time to be friendly and whistle while you work. Have a compliment competition. Spread cheerfulness and warmth throughout your office. Remember the United Airline's tag line "Fly the *friendly* skies" which beckons you back to travel with them for yet another time. Strive to make your office known as "The *friendliest* dental office." Spread good feelings of belonging, companionship, and love. Start today with a big smile, the most contagious and friendly gesture of all.

Chapter 9

ATTITUDE

Serving the customer is my highest calling.
-Dave Sund

Just say YES. Service is an attitude. A Yes! attitude of enthusiasm, teamwork, gratitude, compassion, and empathy creates outstanding customer service. At Gorczyca Orthodontics, we hire our team members based upon their attitude. These attitudes are backed-up by behaviors. We are looking for a Yes! attitude and a demeanor of service.

Attitudes and care with compassion can be developed. The Swartz Center for Compassionate Healthcare (SCCH) in Boston develops programs for compassion training for those in the medical field. They have found that in order for caregivers to provide compassionate care, they themselves must experience a reasonable workload; have autonomy, rewards, and a sense of community with colleagues; feel good about the values of the organization; and have an individual sense of purpose in the value of the work that they do. Perhaps dentists should participate in such a program.

A YES! ATTITUDE

Customer service is a voluntary act that demonstrates the genuine desire to satisfy, if not delight, a customer.
-Steve Curtin

We've already learned that YES is the most powerful word in customer service. Attitude in the office can simply be improved by saying YES. Say YES to your patient's wants and needs, say YES to the doctor's need for assistance, and YES to each other on the dental team. A Yes! attitude is at the core of any successful business.

Each time you say YES, you have an opportunity to make someone's day. Special patient requests for special requests or extra procedures are the customer service playing field of champions. Little things count. It is the sum total of all these small gestures that add up to make a strong and lasting customer service impression that builds brand loyalty.

A service mentality and Yes! attitude include positive words. These phrases would include, "Yes", "Can", "Will do," "Certainly," "My pleasure," "You bet," and "Absolutely." Add to these compliments like "You're great!" "You're awesome!" "You rule!" and "You ROCK!" and you're golden! Make these words and phrases automatically part of your everyday office vocabulary.

A Yes! attitude is eager to please. This customer service leader is excited to help the patient and be a part of the dental team. Service leaders with a Yes! attitude come to work every day with enthusiasm and gratitude, happy to serve the patients. They are great team players and work together with others in harmony. They have empathy for the patients and put the patient first. All of these qualities produce outstanding service, which in turn produces a happy and loyal customer.

Eight Ways to Build a Positive Work Environment

What can we do to help our teams create Yes! attitudes? Research findings from the Schwartz Center for Compassionate Health Care (SCCH) give insight into systemic as well as personal goals important to nurture Yes! attitudes and a positive work environment.

1. Address team member needs so they can focus on taking care of patient needs. Employee happiness drives patient experience.
2. Share patient stories. This will help the dental team to engage and to relate to patients.
3. Hire right. Hire for attitude.
4. Encourage creativity, innovation, and teamwork to create a culture of Yes! attitude.

5. Focus on systems and continuity. Yes! attitude includes the entire team and it is the "secret sauce."
6. Give feedback and share results to inspire excellence. Transparency improves performance.
7. Use simple tactics for quality improvements to enhance the patient experience.
8. Learn to say "Yes!" assume "Yes," and be optimistic. Say "Yes" to others and to yourself.

Four Ways to Always Say "Yes"

Of course, we can't always say "yes." There are times when the answer has to be no. Even so, there are ways to say "no" while still expressing "yes," remaining positive, and maintaining a Yes! attitude. In their book, *The Power of Nice,* authors Linda Kaplan Thaler and Robin Koval outline four ways to say no while still saying yes and having a Yes! attitude. Let's see if we can apply these to the dental office.

1. **"Yes, I want to help you."**

   The patient may ask you to do something you cannot do for either time, ability, or other reasons. Perhaps you can refer the patient to someone who might be able to satisfy this need and keep the positive energy in motion. This might be a great opportunity for another dentist, a dental student, or a specialist. By setting that up, you've made two people happy and you've saved yourself in the process.

2. **"Yes, we can do better."**

   As a boss, we often have to tell people things they don't want to hear. Perhaps you are presented with a monthly report that presents delinquency, or monthly goals have not been met. Rather than saying, "This is terrible," say "We are capable of such terrific work. This is not up to our caliber. Together, we can do better and we start today." Make the necessary changes or corrections and stay positive!

3. **"Yes, I see you."** Small acknowledgements are easy to neglect.

We all have a million things to do, but when you don't respond, you are denying someone's existence. It only takes minutes to respond by e-mail.

I am amazed at the time that the most successful people in the world, CEOs of large corporations and important leaders in dentistry and all professions, take to acknowledge small acts of kindness. They do this personally, on their cell phone, while en route to important engagements and events. A *Wall Street Journal* poll found that thirty-nine out of forty-four surveyed CEOs personally answered e-mails. Take time to say "yes." Are you really busier than Michael Dell?

4. **"Yes, your talent lies elsewhere."**

Once you are beyond the working interview and the ninety-day introductory period for new hires, it is best to not fire an existing employee. If someone is not working out, help them find the right job for their talents. Maybe you can reassign them to a different role in your office. Push them gently in the right direction. Often, if they are not cut out for delivering customer service or working on a team, or in the dental service industry, they will sooner or later discover this on their own and end up quitting dentistry. Wish them well and help them in any way that you can.

Eliminate the Negatives

'No' is a killer word in service.
Never say no to a customer;
everything is negotiable.
-Frank Parenta

"No, we cannot accommodate your request." "No, we cannot see you today." "No, that is not our office policy." By using these phrases you are suggesting that your patient leave your practice, go somewhere where they know how to say yes, and never come back!

In a pinch try, "Let me work on that and see what I can do for you," or "I'll try to accomplish this for you as quickly as possible," or "In the meantime, may I offer you a fresh cup of coffee and a magazine in our reception area?"

Try replacing negative phrases with positive responses. Try:

"Here's what we *can* do for you."

"Let me check."

"Let me find out."

Never tell a customer what you can't do for them unless you immediately follow it with a solution of what you CAN do for them. Eliminate negative responses and phrases whenever possible. Negative words include, "Can't," "Won't," "Don't know," "Not," "Problem," and "Sorry."

Try to identify the killer phrases that you may be using and turn them into positive words of outstanding customer service.

"No" shuts down possibilities while "yes" opens them up. It takes five positive exchanges—yeses, smiles, jokes, compliments, or handshakes—to make up for one negative one. Try to find the good in everything and assume goodwill. Train yourself to experience encounters in a positive way. Be a cheerleader of "yes." Bring a memorable "yes" to everyone you meet to enjoy optimal success.

A NO Attitude

People may hear your words, but they feel your attitude.
-John Maxwell

The word "no" itself sets off a train of negative events. Hearing it immediately dampens one's day. Even if you can't express the "no" feeling generated by a NO attitude, it comes out eventually. Having a NO attitude onboard is a detriment to any dental office and no fun to be around. A NO attitude could be costing your dental office as much as $100,000 to $200,000 per year in income from lost patients. Having a NO attitude with a valued customer who may be already frustrated is sure to send the customer on a journey of no return.

A NO attitude exhibits poor posture and lazy body language. Eyes may be rolling as you hear excuses for lack of personal performance and participation in the delivery of customer service. A YES! attitude keeps the conversation flowing. A NO attitude stops it dead in its tracks.

Customer service is about what you *can do*, not what you can't. Push yourself to say yes when it comes to customer service. Make one last courtesy call. Deliver another customer appreciation gift. Tell your patient, "We're always here for you." Make it a daily goal to do one exceptional customer courtesy each day. Multiply this by everyone on your team and you've assembled a customer service army. Keep personal service alive. A lot can be accomplished with customer service initiatives, which only take a few spare moments each day.

Three Ways to Improve Attitude

For team building, morale, and achievement, it's important to "get off the 'no' train." If a negative attitude is allowed to persist on your team, it will infect others, spread negativity, and decrease productivity. It is extremely important to "nip a 'no' attitude in the bud." There are three ways to turnaround a "no" attitude.

1. **Bring it to the person's attention that they have said "no."**

   They may not realize that they are withdrawing from the team, not willing to do the job that they were hired to do, or that their verbiage is affecting others negatively. If nothing else, give them an opportunity to "snap out of it!" Don't allow "no" to be an acceptable answer at your dental practice.

2. **Have the doctor and the team take the attitude test in Gitomer's Book, *The Little Gold Book of Yes! Attitude.***

   Gitomer's attitude self-test gives each individual a personal attitude score and places them in an attitude category of positive attitude, good, work on attitude, or negative attitude. Specific actions can then be taken to improve or eliminate attitude "bad habits" in order to have a Yes! attitude. Gitomer's *Yes! attitude* book is listed in the bibliography of this text.

   Years ago, I gave the most negative person on my team the task to administering the Gitomer Yes! Attitude Test to our entire team at my team advance. Not only did her less than Yes! attitude improve, the attitude of the entire team improved! I personally learned that I need to refrain from speaking about news in the office, which is usually a negative topic. I like to give this test to my entire team once every few years to remind all of us that we want to be as positive as possible and work with Yes! attitude teammates.

3. **Play a game of improv.**

    One of the important rules of improv is to never say "no." The response must always be "Yes, and…." If you say "no," the improv quickly comes to a stop and you lose.

Try a few office questions to get the game rolling. "Can you come to work early?" "Can we do this one extra dental procedure before lunch?" "Can you take over for me when I'm on vacation?" "Can you help me clean up before you leave for the evening?" You get the idea. I'm sure your team can be creative and get plenty of practice saying "yes" at the same time.

Now try a harder improv question. "Will you marry me on Mars?" If the team member says, "Yes! and we can invite my cousins from Neptune and Pluto!" you'll know you've got a really positive and creative person with an amazing Yes! attitude on your dental team!

Attitude is Everything
Dana, RDA, Records Coordinator

"As records coordinator, each day I have the opportunity to deliver a Yes! attitude to my patients. We offer same-day starts so a new patient can complete their orthodontic records on the same day as their initial exam. This offers the patient an excellent time-saving service. If we have an opening in our schedule, we also take final records at the retainer appointment. It is my responsibility to do as much as I can for the patient that day.

"I have been working as an orthodontic assistant my entire career. What I love most is seeing the transformation in confidence that orthodontic treatment can make. Not only are the patient's teeth straight, healthy, and beautiful, but their overall personality shows more confidence and happiness. It is a wonderful feeling to be part of this life-changing process. Smiles really do change lives!

"When Yes! attitudes are part of the office culture, care, and climate, work-

ing as part of a team becomes more fun. Attendance is reliable and there is a high level of team trust, engagement, and enthusiasm.

"In a stress-free environment, we are able to direct our focus and attention exclusively on the patient. When everyone on the team gets along and is committed, responsible, nice, helpful, and welcoming to the patient and to each other, we are able to deliver the best patient care possible and have the patient journey be a great patient experience."

Chapter 10

ENGAGEMENT

Only the guy who isn't rowing has time to rock the boat.
-Jean-Paul Sartre

Imagine you have a ten-member crewing team. Three members are rowing their butts off. Five members sit idle, while two members are actively attempting to sink the boat. The statistics are shocking. This description coincides with a 2013 Gallup Poll, "State of the American Workplace." The report concluded that only thirty percent of the workforce is engaged. Worse, fifty-two percent are disengaged, while eighteen percent are actively disengaged!

To quickly assess engagement, ask a team member, "What are you thinking about?" If your team member is engaged in the work before them, their response will reflect patient customer service, a task they are responsible for, or a new project that they have initiated in the office. If their response takes you outside of your dental practice, to some personal activity or family concern, it might be time for a refocus. Huddles and meetings are a great way to ignite engagement and build enthusiasm. Take time to recharge the team and build individual team member engagement.

Engaged team members talk about the future of the company with energy and excitement. They're "All In." Focus insures that the right results will happen. Dedicated team members who put patients first successfully obtain better results for the patient. They can't wait to see the patient receive life-changing dental treatment.

Having fully engaged employees is a win-win for the employer and the employee. Enthusiasm and performance raises the productivity level of everyone on the team including the doctor. Engagement also makes the office fun. It makes the team click. Ultimately, it leads to success for everyone involved.

Doctor Engagement

In his book *Uncomplicate Business,* Dr. Howard Farran urges dentists to spend as little time as possible in their private office during patient hours. He suggests that clinical downtime be used as a golden opportunity to bond with customers.

Do not use your "spare" moments to answer your cell phone or surf the web. Social media and texting can wait. Spend time with your patients! For instance, when you are waiting for the local dental anesthetic to set in, instead of sneaking back into your private office, take a moment to ask your patient a question about their life experiences and listen to them. Engage your patient in conversation and create an opportunity to make your customer feel special. The more you know about your patient, such as where they work, where they went to college, what their family is like, and what their hobbies are, the more special they will become, and the more connected you will be. Conversations are where the personalization of excellent customer service starts.

Three Steps of Service Engagement

> *It is the employees who are the principal drivers of customer experience.*
> -Roy Barnes & Bob Kelleher

Engagement begins face-to-face when the patient enters the office front door. All eyes are on the new patient, and everyone says "Hello" during the new patient office tour. The three steps of engagement service which take place at every dental appointment include:

1. *"Welcome Janice. Great to see you today."*

A warm and sincere greeting by name is the first step towards building a relationship and offering service to the new patient.

2. *"What questions do you have for us?"*

Asking an open-ended question is the best way of fulfilling needs and addressing the concerns of the patient and their family. Take time to listen. By asking questions, you are anticipating needs, acknowledging them, and letting the patient know that they matter to you.

3. *"Thank you. We look forward to seeing you again next time."*

A sincere thank you and a fond farewell will be the last impression that the patient and their family have of you and your dental office until the next time that you meet. Make that final impression a memorable one.

Our Team

When we speak of engagement, we begin with our team. It is, after all, your dental assisting team of the service leaders, who drive the customer experience. Engaged team members produce engaged customers. Covering the team side of the customer service experience is therefore critical. To accomplish this, you must first hire great team members with service behaviors and traits who are expressly committed to delivering your outstanding customer service. Don't rush the hiring process.

In my second book, *Beyond the Morning Huddle—HR Management for a Successful Dental Practice,* I review a thirteen-step hiring process. It may take your office as long as a month to find, screen, interview, and hire a friendly customer service leader with a great attitude. Be sure to take the time you need and involve the team in the hiring process to find that additional key player to join your team.

When you interview a new team member candidate, ask yourself, *Are they engaged with what we are doing here? Were they committed to their last job? Why did they leave? Do they have a smile on their face and a great attitude? Will they be an asset to the team and to the office? Do they appear to be ready and eager to serve?*

Jolene is a customer service leader at Gorczyca Orthodontics. Jolene is engaged in her work. Patients ask for her specifically by name. This is the highest compliment any customer service leader can receive. Jolene is a customer service living legend. When it comes to work engagement, Jolene is "all in."

Jolene is a thirty-six-year career veteran who has personally trained over thirty-eight registered dental assistants, helping them to complete their internship and to start their career in the dental field. She also serves on the board of Diablo Valley Junior College, where she studied to become a registered dental assistant in California. She brings her lifetime of experience into play every day for her patients and fellow team members.

Your patient deserves 100 percent of your attention. To achieve this goal, talk less and listen more. Engage in everything that the patient says as if there were a test at the end. Focus on your patient as if your business depended on it. Because it does.

FIVE WAYS TO BUILD TEAM ENGAGEMENT

> *Great customer service is the result of an interaction between an engaged employee and an engaged customer.*
> -Roy Barnes & Bob Kelleher

1. KNOW YOUR OFFICE GOALS

Purpose fuels performance. Clear understanding of office goals and targets give meaning to these tasks. Companies that live their mission, core values, and strategic plan are better able to win with employees who are fully engaged. The more an employee is excited about their own projects, accomplishments, and contribution to success, the higher the likelihood that end results will be achieved.

2. FOSTER A GREAT TEAM ENVIRONMENT

A great employee experience (EX) is the basis for a successful customer experience (CX). If your employees are happy, your customers will be happy. Employee Experience = Customer Experience, EX=CX. The degree to which your team feels cared for will determine their effort in caring for customers. It's that simple.

Great camaraderie, trust, friendship, respect, and love are engaging. It's great to have a best friend at work and to be surrounded by people you look forward to being with. Be an office where people look forward to coming to work each and every day.

3. HAVE A BOSS-EMPLOYEE RELATIONSHIP

Like it or not, one of the drivers of employee engagement is an employee's relationship with his or her boss. Building in-office and out-of-office relationships are where it starts. Off-sites, team meetings, and office celebrations build the boss-employee relationship and increase communication and understanding, which fuel engagement at work. As the leader, show your team members that you are human. Show your vulnerability and build trust. Be open and honest about all concerns you have about the office and areas which need improvement. Show your team that you are human, honest, and engaged.

4. CREATE ENGAGEMENT BRANDING

Emphasize your brand of customer service leaders. Highlight and recognize your customer service leaders individually. Let them know why each one of them matters. Feature team members and their accomplishments whenever you can. Capture your employees' heads and hearts. True engagement comes when there is a personal and emotional connection with the dental office.

5. HAVE FUN

Laughter is often the first sign of a great work environment. People are happy and allowed to express who they are and what they love. Fun and enjoyment make for a healthy workplace.

Have team members talk about their personal events at huddles and gatherings. Create some teamwork games, awards, and recognition. Have a bonus system. These are sure ways to incorporate the team into projects that matter for office success.

CUSTOMER RELATIONS MANAGEMENT

*Up to 80% of your total revenue is driven by referrals,
so it is critical to not only identify, but also nurture your advocates.*
-Dana Severson

Customer Relations Management (CRM) is the customer service frontier. It is customer relations engagement. Digital social media has transformed CRM and made its activity more transparent both inside and outside the office. Most new patient communication now takes place by text messaging on a cell phone. This is the evolution of customer service. Offices that are able to seamlessly blend online communities so as to assist customer service before, during, and after a dental appointment will have a competitive advantage.

Data shows that the healthcare service industry is not very social. Sprout Social reports that healthcare ranks fifteenth out of fifteen when it comes to brand engagement ranking. That's dead last! Response time to patient inquiries and questions on social media was low: 10.2 hours. Engagement was low at 20.1 posts per reply.

Why is this? It is not recommended that physicians give advice in the Internet forum. There can be liability associated with answers given to patients in writing on the Internet. For physicians and even dentists, the best answer is often "Please come and see me in the office and I will be happy to answer all of your questions."

Increased social media promotions may be decreasing customer engagement. Perhaps dentists are over saturating the social media space. Perhaps dentists post too often. Social Sprout rates the healthcare sector customer engagement at seventh out of fifteen industries. Perhaps dentists need to be strategic and targeted when it comes to online presence.

There's no doubt, people love their smart phones! People live for social engagement. Directly highlighting patients through social media is one of the most effective ways to drive reposting and sharing, resulting in new referrals. Be equipped to answer appropriate social engagement questions in four hours or less for your dental office. Be responsive! Nothing beats immediate engagement in the form of a caring response that is individualized. When you show some interest and personality, social media will become part of your CRM brand.

ENGAGE YOUR TEAM IN CRM

In order for patients to be engaged with your practice, you will need to be engaged with your patients. With CRM, you are engaged with your patients one-on-one, every step of the way along the customer experience journey. Map out every customer engagement check point. Keep record of areas of delight and increase them. Record and review areas that need a tune-up and focus on making these interaction areas of delight as well.

It's easy to engage your team members in your customer service program. Give each one an individual and specific customer service task. External activities could include office decorations, contests, prizes, kid's club, Facebook photos, patient rewards programs, Yelp reviews, theme weeks, or asking for customer feedback. Internal efforts could include reviewing scripts of office facts, niceties, or public relations messages that you would like to make known to your patients and the public. If your team members are engaged in the CRM process, your patient interactions will flourish. Your customers will feel your culture, care, and climate. You will have achieved customer service success.

Social Media

People's Top Choices for Customer Care
34% Social Media
24.7% Website/Live Chat
19.4% Email
16.1% Phone
5.3% On Site
     -Sprout Social

Ninety percent of customers use social media in some way to communicate with a brand. In 2016, a study by Sprout Social revealed customers' top choices for customer care. Social media easily surpassed phone and e-mail as the number one choice. Social media simply offers urgent and immediate feedback.

Chances are that your new customer, the dental patient, has already checked you out online. They will have visited sites like Yelp (www.yelp.com), Google places (www.googleplaces.com), Facebook (www.facebook.com), Twitter (www.twitter.com), or LinkedIn (www.linkedin.com.) As a first step in online reputation management, "Google" the following: "Your Practice Name, Reviews". Read *all* customer feedback. This is what your new patients are seeing!

Customers aren't the only ones talking about your office online. It is possible that your employees are doing it as well. In this digital age, it is important for all employees to understand that what they say online can either build the practice's reputation or be a poor reflection of your practice culture. Many employers now prefer to review social media sites of potential employees, before an interview. This is a great way to evaluate if a new team member is a good fit for your office. It's an instant background check.

As an employer, it makes me very uncomfortable to have a team member *unwilling* to be my friend on Facebook. We want team members who are the same good people and citizens both in and out of the office. If someone is unwilling to publicly share aspects of their personal life beyond privacy issues, it makes we wonder, *What are they hiding? What are they doing? What don't they want their office to know about?*

I once had an employee who left Gorczyca Orthodontics to go work in another orthodontic office. She started writing derogatory remarks on Facebook about the new doctor and new office. She had been my Facebook friend for a while in our office without complication. But when I contacted her to let her know that her social media comments were damaging to her new employer, she unfriended me! Needless to say, she did not remain in this new office long.

Negativity of all types is damaging to both you and your dental office. Posting thoughts like, "I couldn't wait for this day to be over" sends a poor message into the community about you. Lack of positivity and uplifting posts in social media are unfair to your patients, your place of employment, and your social media community. If an employee truly feels negatively about dentistry, perhaps they are in the wrong profession.

Social Media Customer Engagement

Without social,
it's just media.
          -Sprout Social

Without engagement, social media is just another website. Make sure your social media sites are up to date, and that you are engaging with your patients online in an ongoing, real-time way.

A 2016 study by Sprout Social revealed that customers consider under four hours reasonable for a social media response time, and that thirty percent of people will go to a competitor if a brand does not respond to their social media inquiry. Done well, your iPhone will replace a pager or answering service for immediate patient feedback. It is important to note that you do not need to respond to a social media inquiry via social media. For clinically-related matters, for instance, replying via social messaging is *not* advised, for reasons of confidentiality or HIPAA compliance. But, you can address a texted question by having a staff member (or even the doctor) call back immediately, via cell phone. A *timely* personal response is the most important thing and the power and benefit of social media initial contact.

The good news is that seventy-five percent of people are likely to share a good experience on their own social media profile. The payback or ROI (return on investment) with social media is huge. Here, outstanding customer service can heighten and grow with your public relations activities and community outreach programs to grow your practice. Making meaningful connections with your patients and your community on social media in real time is the current marketing wave now, and this trend will only continue to grow in the future.

YELP

Unless you have 100% customer satisfaction,
you must improve.
-Horst Schulz

Customer service appears to have the strongest effect on reviews. There is probably no site as important for the evaluation of customer service as Yelp. If you can make it there, you'll make in anywhere. Yelp's research has found that a customer whose review praises "customer service" is five times more likely to give a five-star review than a one-star review. Either ask your patients for customer service feedback in person and make continuous improvements, or read about your deficits on Yelp. Nearly seventy percent of those who trash a business' customer service wind up giving a one-star review on Yelp.

Make five-star reviews a customer service goal. Yelp believes in quality over quantity. Darnell Holloway, Yelp's Manager of Local Business Outreach, says that perception still lingers that restaurants are Yelp's biggest category because reviews for the food service industry are far more ubiquitous as compared to, for example, dentistry. "We recommend that people focus on awareness," letting customers know that the business is on Yelp, "rather than asking for reviews," says Holloway.

Everything is more believable when it comes from a trusted source. For good or bad, social media affects patient trust. Shared in real time, your social media, Facebook, Google+, Yelp, and other sites may bring you new patients or drive them away. Social media is your brand. If your social media presence shows that you care, through the quality of your posts and your responses to actual patients, it will therefore help to build your practice.

A study by Michael Luca, a professor at the Harvard Business School, found that there was a correlation between a high Yelp ranking and revenues. A trusted peer review is worth its weight in gold. Yelp is the new phone book. Don't ignore it. Yelp is ground zero for building new patient trust. The present economy is built on a trust network, and Yelp is often where trust starts.

Take time to look at your Yelp reviews, study them, and share them with your team. This exercise can not only be a sense of joy and pride for your team members, but also be a great informational resource for customer service improvements.

SHARE THE GOOD NEWS

*Customer service represents the heart of a brand
in the hearts of its customers.*
-Kate Nasser

Check out your customer reviews. Categorize comments. See what you can learn and improve.

I took time to go through my twenty-one customer service reviews on Yelp. Here's what patients from Gorczyca Orthodontics had to say:

> Place: Patient Experience
> "The office is very clean and comfortable."
> "The office is always cheerfully decorated."
> "I'm thrilled with the service I received there."
> "Best run office I've been to."

Product: Things Patients Love
"Super nice and fun!"
"I'm very happy with my treatment."
"OMG it was awesome!"
"I give them an A+."

Price: Dental Care Affordability
"Prices are reasonable."
"Easy payment options."
"Finishing up our third kid. All experiences have been great."

Promotion: Patient Experience
"I couldn't be happier."
"I will refer… to Gorczyca Orthodontics ;)!"
"You are definitely #1 in my book."

The Team
"The staff has repeatedly gone the extra mile."
"Amazing and talented group of people."
"High standard of professionalism."

The Doctor
"Dr. Gorczyca always takes time to listen."
"She is about patients and their individual needs."
"Friendly, helpful, and compassionate."
"Dr. Gorczyca is fantastic."
"She's the best orthodontist EVER!"

Customer feedback is a gift that will continue to inspire and motivate both the doctor and your customer service team. Don't delay doing this essential exercise for your dental office. It will give you insight into the public's perception of your office brand.

Now the Bad News

> *The customer's perception
> is your reality.*
> -Kate Zabriskie

Collect your bad news. I hope you have none. I'd like to think that we all have only five-star reviews. At the time of writing this book, our office did, except for one. What can we learn from this one three-star review?

What I learned was that all patients, regardless of their age, need to be asked, "Is there anything more we can do for you?" All patient insights, even when coming from a thirteen-year-old patient, are of the utmost importance. Collect and record all feedback. Every comment will only help your office to improve.

When reviewing your customer service feedback, ask yourself the following questions:
What have we learned?
What change have we made?
What new systems and processes do we need to add?

The Future of Online Reviews

Present-day surveys and reviews online allow to you address emotions, comments, and complaints in a timely manner. This feedback gives you the opportunity to address individual needs, to call the patient, and to give them what they need and want. Take time to listen to patient concerns, apologize when necessary, and fix their problems. Don't miss this golden opportunity.

If you have negative reviews from strangers on Yelp or other social media sites, hire a private investigator through an attorney. Identify the source. Unknown reviews may come from your competition or a disgruntled, dismissed employee. The source may surprise you. It is certainly not in your best interest to allow false reviews to exist.

In the future, customers will be able to seek reviews from known individuals from within their own social media network. These will be trusted reviews from known family and friends, and this will be a valued future referral base of new patients for your dental practice.

Chapter 11

SMILE

*Your smile is your logo, your personality is your business card,
how you leave others feeling after having an experience
with you becomes your trademark.*
-Jay Danzie

The American norm of customer service is "Service with a smile." If you hire people who are happy, love patients, enjoy their work, and smile, you can't go wrong. Like yawning, when you smile, chances are the people around you will smile back. A smile is an expression of happiness. Hire team members who love delivering customer service and constantly smile, and your patients will smile and be happier. Now you've got a winning customer service experience.

Happiness

What makes you smile? Is it your child, your boyfriend, your puppy? Put a picture of what makes you smile at your desk. Joyful reminders will make you smile each morning when you enter your dental office. "Walls of happiness" inside closet doors remind you of what you love about your job and career. Play the song "Happy" on your drive to the office. Whatever your mind thinks, your day will become. Your mental state will manifest in your body language and attitude. Give yourself a reason to smile. Be happy and make other people happy!

Our thoughts, outlooks, and imagination can greatly enhance or inhibit our smiles. Our charisma and friendliness are revealed by our smiles towards other people. It is not possible to fake a heartfelt smile. Really mean it! A real smile will cause your eyes to twinkle, changing the expression of your entire face. When the love of customer service and dentistry is not real, smiling becomes a chore. A fake smile will only involve your mouth, teeth, and lips. Smile naturally and from the bottom of your heart.

You can't teach people to smile. New team members have to smile before you hire them. You also can't make your team happy. They have to be internally happy before you hire them. If they are happy people, they will be smiling. It's that easy.

If your patient comes to your dental office without a smile, give them one of yours. To make your patients smile, you will need to smile yourself first. This is where an attitude of "It's Showtime!" comes in. Teach yourself to smile. Take a minute to smile at the start of each work day. Change "It's Showtime!" to "It's Smile Time!" Smiling is contagious. When you smile at your patients and each other, people will smile back.

Health Benefits of Smiles

Sometimes your joy is the source of your smile.
Sometimes your smile is the source of your joy.
-Thich Nhat Hahn

A 2012 study found that people who smile experienced less stress and more positive emotions. Research has even shown that artificially reducing the ability to frown with Botox may help to relieve depression. Not only does smiling feel good, it's good for your mental and physical health.

Smiling produces vocal warmth. People can hear the smile in your voice. Smiling affects how we speak. A study by Amy Drahota showed that a listener can determine sixteen different kinds of smiles based on sound alone. Excitement, engagement, caring, and friendliness can be expressed by a smile and even over the phone, the listener can "hear" the smile in your voice. Smile when you walk into the initial exam room. We're in the smile business, after all!

Telephone Etiquette

> *I will keep smiling,*
> *be positive and never give up!*
> *I will give 100 percent*
> *each time I play.*
> *These are always my goals*
> *and my attitude.*
> -Yani Tseng

Telephone smiling comes with specific challenges. Place a small mirror at the front desk right by the reception telephone and before answering the phone, instruct your team to take a split second, stop what they are doing, smile, and then answer the phone.

Not only do we need to smile when answering the phone, but we want the caller to smile as well.

You need good timing for good results. Always put the customer first when making phone calls. Ask, "Is this a good time for you?" Busy patients appreciate your thoughtfulness.

Being present on the phone for the new patient call is even more important than it is in person. Listen to what is going on in the background of the phone call. If you hear children's voices, you may need to politely ask if there is a better time to talk. Assure the person on the line that if they need to take care of family matters at this time, that's OK, you will wait. The caller will appreciate your sensitivity to their needs, especially if the caller is a busy mom.

Calling back new exams to start treatment is critical to our dental practice success. It may determine the growth of your practice. Pay attention to what the new patient is saying. Focus on the customer as if you were face-to-face. Don't get distracted. To avoid interruptions, if necessary, hold up a colored sign that reads, "This is an important new customer. Do not disturb!" No other interruption or activity should be going on while you are speaking with a patient on the phone.

If you are having trouble focusing, close your eyes. Block out all noise and distractions beyond the sound of your patient's voice. If needed, go to a room and close the door. Give your patient your undivided attention.

Warning: do not eat or drink while talking on the phone. This practice is very unprofessional. A caller can hear you chewing and swallowing because receivers amplify sound. Instruct your team to take their breaks out of the office to eat lunch. This is also good for mental health, and a half-hour break is the law!

Caution: stop typing! Do not word process as you gather patient information over the phone! People can hear you typing. It causes patients to wonder why your receptionist responds like a robot, not really paying attention to them. While typing, the delayed voice response and slowed speech patterns sound non-empathetic. Stay human and carry on a conversation.

Author Leil Lowndes recommends answering calls in a crisp and professional voice. After you hear who is calling, let warmth, friendship, and enthusiasm sound through your voice. Make the caller feel special, like a VIP, or the most important person in the room. This is what professional customer service departments practice. They claim that the gains with this technique are impressive. Keep score of new exams to treatment starts. This will be your phone call to new patient conversion rate. Your office computer system can also track new patient calls, new patient exams, and new patient starts. Many computer systems provide graphics for you to track this metric, or one applicable to your office or subspecialty.

WE MAKE YOU SMILE

If you want to make a good first impression, smile at people.
What does it cost not to smile?
Everything, if not smiling prevents you from enchanting people.
-Guy Kawasaki

Our patients visit our dental offices each day with a wide range of emotional needs. These issues are often expressed to the dentist and the dental team. Having empathy and understanding is truly what it means to be a healthcare provider.

Last week, a patient came into my office for what she perceived as an orthodontic emergency. She expressed that her maxillary right second bicuspid was too high in occlusion, and she was concerned that it was not erupting fast enough to accommodate her imminent move to another state. I took the detailed orthodontics arch wire out and put in a .014 Niti over the tooth bracket with an up-down elastic to pull it down. I told the patient I was putting her on turbo charge, and that she needed to sit with us for a while as the tooth extruded right then and there in the chair. She sat with us in the treatment bay for one and a half hours, watching her tooth while other patients came and went.

During this time, the patient shared with us how scared she was about her upcoming move. This was something she needed to do alone with her son, as her husband was in service to our country. She poured out her emotional needs. By the end of the day, the patient looked great. More importantly, she felt great. She needed a little TLC (tender loving care). She needed to feel that she was not alone in her life struggle.

It's at times like these that we need to remind ourselves that we are in business to serve the patient, whatever "serve" means. Sometimes serving will include emotional support; sometimes it means listening; and sometimes it means being a friend. Whatever the situation, you can be there to help your patient smile by active listening, by being empathetic, and by using the words, "You are important to us."

Sometimes, however, it becomes necessary to remind the patient, "We don't treat feelings, we treat teeth." This is important when patients project their feelings on to their teeth. An example might be a patient saying, "I feel my teeth are a certain way" when the dentist may not agree. This is why speaking in pictures is so important in dentistry. Looking at the patient's clinical pictures together and having the patient point to "what they feel" is helpful. Whatever the situation, the point is always to give satisfaction and enjoyment to the patient experience, having your patient leave with a smile.

A sincere smile works wonders. You can create a patient smile in many ways. Verbal smiling is giving a compliment. Telling your patient that they look nice or dress well will make them smile. Telling them that you are happy to see them, how much they mean to you, or how special they are to your dental office and dental team will also make them smile. Making your patients feel special, loved, and appreciated will put a smile on their face.

Surprises and gifts also produce smiles. A new toothbrush, a tube of toothpaste, floss, mouthwash, or a new oral hygiene bundle from Crest Oral B will make them smile. With these items, you can give your patients the gift of oral health and make them smile at the same time!

Joy

> *We shall never know all the good*
> *that a simple smile can do.*
> -Mother Teresa

An environment of joy affects not only your office success but your personal health and the well-being of every member of your team. The service of healthcare can take a personal toll on our health. Days may be stressful. Dealing with the public is full of daily challenges. Besides remembering to smile, be sure to care for yourself. Sleep well, exercise, get outside, eat healthily, and stand up straight. All of these small personal efforts will contribute to your personal joy that cannot help but accrue to the benefit of your office and your patients.

Mindfulness

Harvard researcher Michael Porter outlined three key areas of happiness in his "Social Progress Index" as being healthcare, food, and education. You, as a healthcare provider, are helping your patients improve themselves to be happier. What could be better than that? Ask your patients what aspect of your office makes them happy. Whatever they answer, do more of that.

Be mindful of the level of team happiness. One unhappy person on the team can be a total downer for everyone in the office. Patients want to see smiling and happy team members and doctors. Customers feel at ease when the atmosphere is pleasant and unrushed, with team members exhibiting confident, positive, body language. We're in the smile business. Smiles change lives. Let your smiles shine!

Fun

> *I never did a day's work in my life. It was all fun.*
> -Thomas A. Edison

Fun activities build your patient experience. Try starting a "We make you smile" campaign or a contest in which team members and patients can engage. A never-ending assortment of fun patient campaigns is available from My Social Practice. Find them at www.mysocialpractice.com.

Campaigns, contests, and entertainment for your patients can be a delightful surprise. You may want to give out patient reward tokens for visiting your office, wearing your T-shirt, having no cavities, or being on time. We still use wooden tokens that can be exchanged for physical prizes on display. Kids can also visit a toy box as a reward for good behavior. A teenager might like to exchange their tokens for movie passes. Adults deserve prizes, too. Gift cards or event tickets are always appreciated.

You can decorate your office for holidays or for an event. Keep up with the times and join current world events, such as the Olympics. Kids can join an office Kids' Club that encourages participation in special contests and events. Appreciation parties or Kids' Day are enjoyable for the whole office.

Decorations and themes will delight your patients in every way. These extra efforts and expressions of customer service keep your patients and team engaged, mindful, and involved in receiving a unique patient experience.

Chapter 12

APPEARANCE

*You only get one chance
to make a great first impression.*
-Anonymous

Books have been written about professional appearance, dressing for success, and making a good first impression. In my book, *Beyond the Morning Huddle—HR Management for a Successful Dental Practice*, I describe in detail dress code for the dental office. As team leader and creator of office culture, care, and climate, you have the authority to enforce a high standard of dress code, as outlined in your Team Handbook. Maintenance of the dress code will be your responsibility.

Body language and appearance reflect status and confidence. Give time and attention to having everyone on your team, including the doctor, looking good. Your appearance counts. Your authority as a doctor or as a dental professional depends on how confident you feel, and how you look at that key moment when you greet a new patient.

Dental assistants or customer service leaders should have a uniform that is clean, pressed, and in good condition. Male dentists should be carefully groomed. Female dentists should also take time with their hair, as well as make-up tastefully done. Don't overdo cologne or perfume as patients can be sensitive or even allergic.

Posture and professional speech also count. Stand up straight. Take care not to hunch over. Stretch your shoulders back. A quick exercise to achieve a chest opening position is to turn your palms forward when you stand. Good posture will not only look good, but it will be a healthier work-posture long-term. This is especially important for work longevity in dentistry.

Eliminate non-verbal reassurances such as nodding or fidgeting. Speak less. Speak slowly and distinctly, with good diction. Don't rush. Look your patients in the eye, and take time to listen. Then ask questions.

A Professional Look

Patients will be forming an opinion of you within the first seven seconds of entering your dental office. You want everyone on your team to look professional and capable. You only get one chance to make a great first impression.

Everyone on your team needs to be smart and look smart. A team of high performers who push towards excellence will look and feel confident. Their combined appearance needs to express the level of excellence of the team. Everyone needs to feel comfortable at work and feel that they belong. A dress code and selection of team uniforms will accomplish unity.

Take the time to maintain your clothing. Pants will need to be hemmed and shoes shined. Jewelry must be minimal. Maintain a professional appearance of fingernails, with standard length just at the tips of the fingers, so as to not stab a patient during treatment.

The goal is to dress well. Choosing clothing that is high quality is one of the easiest ways to look authoritative. Don't be over-dressed, but do look professional.

What Patients "See"

What do patients notice first about your personal appearance? Forty-seven percent will remember your smile. A smaller percentage will notice the scent not only of the human being closest to them but also of the dental office. Make sure your personal being has an attractive fragrance. Your clothes are noticed by seven percent of your patients. Lastly, your hairstyle will catch their eye.

Appearance Killers

*If you think professional is expensive,
wait until you try amateur!*
-Paul Adair

Picture in your mind the world's worst receptionist. Her uniform and hair are sloppy. She is wearing too much make-up. She's chewing gum and rolling her eyes while having her feet up on the front desk. She's eating food while answering the phone. Her attitude is inattentive. Her posture is poor. She makes patients wait while she conducts her personal business. Her actions are rude. Worst of all, she couldn't care less.

Don't let your dress code go "Helter Skelter." Remember that everyone in dentistry is in the business of healthcare service. Our service is one of assistance and hospitality. Everyone needs to take pride in their personal appearance, actions, and behaviors. If your team does not enjoy caring for people and paying attention to the smallest of personal details, then dentistry may not be the place for them.

Uniforms

*When we feel good about our appearance,
it reflects in our overall well-being.*
-Debora Carrier, RDH

Just as a basketball team wears a uniform, an office uniform signifies unity and fosters spirit and a sense of belonging. Uniforms look professional and are always a sign of a well-controlled office and an aligned team. Work uniforms instill a sense of pride and responsibility, turning team members into instant "brand ambassadors." Uniforms are cost-effective, time-saving, and an appreciated employee benefit.

Uniforms create an attractive business image and promote the office brand. A well-designed logo worn in public is a "walking billboard" for your practice. Uniforms immediately identify your valued team members; name tags add a personal and professional touch, helping patients to interact with everyone in your office.

Uniforms offer functional benefits, such as being a safety barrier. This clothing needs to be comfortable: warm when needed and cool when necessary. Registered dental hygienist Debora Carrier has created a uniform that allows her to stay warm and move freely while still looking good. Her uniforms, found at www.twiceasniceuniforms.com, come with removable liners for added comfort. Available for dentists, dental assistants, and hygienists, these scrubs and lab coats bring comfort to those who bring comfort to others in the dental industry.

Uniform Maintenance

Dental team uniforms tend to deteriorate a bit more than personal clothing. Since uniforms are purchased by the dental office, take time to inspect the uniforms on a regular basis. Buy high quality new uniforms at least once per year. Office wear needs to be clean, pressed, and properly fit, neither tight nor baggy. Uniforms need to be color coordinated, and not faded or worn. When appropriate, shirts should be tucked, with ties, scarves, and necklaces and bracelets kept out of harm's way.

Camera Ready

In this era of social media, we are constantly having our picture taken. Prepare to have your office photo taken each day. Cameras do not lie. Our actual appearance is revealed, and areas that need to be improved can be addressed.

Appearance is just one important way to show respect and appreciation to your patients. Appearance counts. Your goal is to have your entire office look clean, healthy, and professional.

You're trying to instill patient confidence in your capabilities. Your appearance shows how much you care about yourself, your patients, your job, and the success of your office. Take time to perfect your professional appearance, image, and customer service brand. How you look and portray yourself counts. For assistance in the area of brand image and wardrobe, contact Janice Hurley at www.janicehurleycom.

Chapter 13

IMPRESSION

Our work is the presentation of our abilities.
-Edward Gibbon

Try to see, feel, and interact with your dental office as if it were for the very first time. Walk in the front door and experience your office from the new patient's perspective. By completing this exercise, you'll never look at your dental office the same way again.

That Wow! Moment

Think back to a time when you were a child and you met the first person whose occupation really impressed you. Perhaps it was an airline pilot, teacher, or fireman. You were in complete awe. You can probably remember the environment, the uniform, the friendly smile, the attention accorded you, sights, and the sounds of the experience as though it were yesterday. You looked back at your parents and said, "I want to be like him one day! I want to do this work. I love it!"

This was my experience with my own orthodontist, Dr. Larry Oliveira of New Bedford, Massachusetts. He had a beautiful new office. It had a saltwater fish tank. His personal office had plush brown carpet. I remember admiring it as he explained the orthodontic treatment plan to my parents in the room in which they signed the financial contract for orthodontic treatment. Dr. Oliveira always looked and smelled great. Even his breath smelled good like the Cepacol mouthwash that he always had in the office. He was a thoughtful and caring man. He even called me on my birthday! I couldn't believe it! All I could say was, "Wow!"

Acting the Part

Make the customer the star of the show.
-Scott McKain

At Disneyland, they call it "Rehearsing the Show"—preparing a part so that excellent customer service can be achieved on a consistent basis. Practice doesn't make perfect; it simply makes good service a habit. To be a customer service star, you must learn the part, deliver the performance, and always strive to improve.

How well you present yourself and your dental office to your patient is clearly an essential component of your success. Once you enter the office, "It's Showtime!" We must be constantly ready for the show to begin.

A patient's view of your office starts with internal marketing. This includes all aspects of the patient experience, from the first phone call to the last impression, which comes from the patient's farewell from your office. Everything which you present to the patient reflects your clinical skills and the level of care you provide. Presentation success doesn't automatically happen. You must carefully and methodically plan your part.

Patients should not know if you're not feeling well, if you're tired, or if you have some type of personal problem. It should not be apparent to patients that you're one team member short or that a piece of dental equipment isn't working properly. Urgent add-on patients should not impede their routine office visits. Disruptions should not be part of their customer service experience.

Your customers are looking for happy, cheerful, skilled, attentive, and positive dental team members, and a fabulous dentist to personally take great care of them. They are seeking clinical excellence, outstanding customer service, and a great patient experience.

If someone on your dental team is having a bad day, you have two choices: address and change the behavior or send the person home. Your business is customer service. Put your show face on. The show must go on!

Acting the part of a customer service leader makes customers feel comfortable. Customer service delivery relieves patient stress and builds trust and confidence in your ability to deliver outstanding patient care.

SCRIPTING

Ninety percent of spiels at Disney are scripted. Nothing is left to chance. These scripts are so well-known and learned that they become personalized and owned as they are repeated again and again. It can be the same for you in your dental office. Does your team have the customer service training that they need in order to say and do the right thing to deliver outstanding customer service? Scripting can help.

BUILDING THE PATIENT EXPERIENCE

We can't treat our customers (on the outside)
any better than we treat each other on the inside.
-Jim Williams

Cross-training is critical in the delivery of outstanding customer service. First and foremost, your dental office needs to make business transactions easy. Every team member benefits by understanding and respecting all office jobs. When all tasks are done with ease, it improves work flow, and the new patient overall impression. Cross-training leads to dental office success.

One special dental team member stays connected with them through the start of treatment. This person is the "Treatment Coordinator." She takes care of the new patient and answers all of their questions. She is always available. Once the treatment has started, the Treatment Coordinator gives a warm transfer to the clinical assistants and doctor for patient care. The Treatment Coordinator should be the most trusted and crucial member of your dental team. She critically is responsible for getting to YES.

If team members are treated well, customers will be treated well. If team members are trusting, accountable, cross-trained, and respectful of each other and the doctor, team members will be polite to customers.

Everyone needs to be "all in" in service to the customer. Each member of your team needs to avoid working within their own silos, limiting themselves to their own expertise. Everyone on the team must work together as an effective and efficient organization. Proficiency as a team includes passing the customer service experience back and forth with anticipation, choreographing every move in the interest of patient care.

Surprises

> *Remember: No matter how good your feedback is,*
> *you always start over with the next customer.*
> -Shep Hyken

We all become accustomed to our daily routines and everyday schedules. We sometimes forget to appreciate that on this one special day, our new patient will step foot into our dental office for the very first time. To them, it is like a blind date. We want this first encounter to progress to a healthy relationship.

Look at your office as if it were for the very first time. Imagine it is the first day you opened. Everything is new and fresh. All first impressions are great and lasting. You are sharp and at the top of your game. Now you are ready to welcome your new patient for the very first time.

Surprises can be a great way to amaze and delight your customers. An unexpected care call from the doctor is one example. It takes but a few moments and it costs you nothing. A phone call from the doctor is heartfelt, and builds trust. The return on investment is infinite.

Keeping the office fresh is not always easy. Seasonal decorations, flowers, and other accents can help in an effort to be constantly interesting. Monthly campaigns or team service projects are another way to keep the office lively and the team engaged, ensuring that everyone, including the patient, is having fun.

The fondest of farewells at the end of treatment is the most important impression of all. Your patient will carry this feeling of the day their braces came off, or the day that the bridge or implant was delivered, for a lifetime. Make it a memorable and special day. We only have one opportunity to build a positive patient memory for life.

Lasting Impressions

> *Be somebody*
> *who makes everybody*
> *feel like somebody.*
> -Robby Novak

Impressions add up. We could call this your dental brand. This is where front-line service meets marketing and sales. Good impressions add to your patient's happiness. Like all of us, customers want to be treated as sensitive human beings. They are not a "case" or a "start." They are people. They are our friends. They have feelings, emotions, and dreams.

Appoint a chief customer officer (CCO)—one person who is responsible for overseeing, focusing, and ensuring that your patients enjoy a great customer service experience in your dental office and manage the customer experience journey, step by step, in its entirety. Show how much you care.

Part III

CLIMATE

We see our customers as invited guests to a party,
and we are the hosts.
It's our job every day to make every important aspect
of the customer experience a little bit better.
-Jeff Bezos

It's going to be a bright, bright, sunshiny day! This is the climate we strive for at Gorczyca Orthodontics. What is your office climate? Is it balmy, pleasant, bright, and sunny, or rainy, stormy, hot, and cold? You decide each and every day what your office climate will be. You create it.

Do you and your dental team believe in your hearts and minds that you are making the world a better place? Do you feel that what you do is important and that people are counting on you for their well-being and dental health? Your customers need you, look forward to seeing you, and appreciate what you do. What you do for a living, by working in dentistry, is extremely important to the successful lives of your patients. You could even save a life. It is indeed a privilege to be able to help your patients, your customers, in such an important way. This fulfillment ultimately leads to enjoyment and pride. Look for the self-satisfaction, passion, and fun within your own work. Reflect this fulfillment in your office climate.

Your climate may be described as relaxing and friendly, or efficient and high tech. Each dental climate should be designed to appeal to your unique communities. Ask your patients to describe the climate in your dental office. See if their perception is the climate that you are striving to achieve.

CLIMATE

Climate may be described as everything the customer feels about a business. The customer may feel special, like a newly engaged couple at Tiffany's. They might feel thrilled like a child at Disneyland. Whatever it is, your climate will reflect your brand.

Your climate can be monitored, measured, and adjusted to respond to patient feedback. Just like air temperature in your office, you can adjust your customer service dials for your desired climate result.

Chapter 14

EMPOWERMENT

There is nothing that harvests more of a feeling of empowerment than being of service to someone in need.
-Gillian Anderson

Empowerment means getting the job done. Front-line customer service leaders are approved by management to handle the customer's need in the present moment. Resolve the request immediately and deliver five-star customer service.

Each customer service leader is empowered to do whatever it takes to make the office the best that it can be through immediate delivery of customer care. Improvement of your management systems will reduce customer requests.

Your Team

People are acknowledged as the organization's greatest assets.
-Dan Sanders

Imagine that you are the captain of a crew team. Seated in the shell on the river, the team members put their oars into the water to compete in an important regatta. The race begins. Suddenly, one team member stops rowing. The other team members row even harder and faster in an effort to keep up. Then, one team member drops their oar into the water and actually rows backwards, working against the team. At this point, the team obviously cannot win the important race and it's time for the captain to make some important changes.

In your quest to build a customer-center culture, you will soon realize the importance of each team member. One unengaged or ill-suited member can ruin all of your team efforts. The underperforming player will need to be coached to quickly improve, placed on the bench, or perhaps even cut from the team. This is perhaps the most difficult management task in building the engagement needed for a five-star customer service team.

Competence is a necessity. We recruit and maintain team members who exhibit good citizenship behaviors. We must eliminate those with poor attendance, bad attitude, or sub-par performance so as to maintain and build customer service excellence.

The Four Cs of Customer Service

It isn't making mistakes that is critical;
it's correcting them and getting on with the principal task.
-Donald Rumsfeld

By Collecting, Compiling, Correcting, and Communicating customer office data, you will be able to systematically reduce and eliminate management system problems. Keep a log of mishaps. Once you do, you can address and correct these actions permanently. This is the hard work of customer service.

In order for your office to run like a well-oiled machine, your team must be empowered to handle any minor need or complaint on a moment's notice. Yet, sometimes dirt, pebbles, or human carelessness, or just plain neglect or apathy slows down your customer service engine. With coaching and training, team members must be capable of performing their duties so well that mistakes don't happen in the first place.

Before we enable the team with a sense of empowerment, it's important to review a few rules of customer service. These are actions service leaders need to adopt to keep patients and customers happy.

1. COLLECTING

In my first book *It All Starts with Marketing—201 Marketing Tips for a Successful Dental Practice*, I tell the story of a response I once received on my customer survey:

"Doctor Gorczyca, I love your office but the National Geographic films in the reception area have got to go!"

The office videos and movies then changed to TV. Patients can now change the channel and watch what they wish. This is especially popular during the World Series and World Cup Soccer.

Another response read:

"You have no magazines for men. I suggest *Cycling*."

We immediately bought *Cycling* magazine and gave an extra copy to our patient with a note of thanks.

How are you going to respond when you get constructive criticism? Are you going to say "Thank you, thank you VERY much," or are you going to be insulted? The customer is your boss and feedback is a gift. Why not make your boss happier?

Written comments are worth their weight in gold. Some comments may need a phone call from the doctor. If a patient has waited too long for their appointment, they may need an apology. If something has gone wrong, and you were not able to deliver on a promise, this patient will need a gift card or special attention with your personal guarantee that their inconvenience will never happen again.

Most dental office websites offer the functionality of an online survey. Be sure that your front desk prints these electronic surveys on a regular basis and presents them at the team meeting. Take a hard look at your survey responses. Keep track and keep score. Make sure problems are resolved and eliminated.

2. COMPILING

The leader of customer loyalty, The Ritz-Carlton, has set a target of an "error-free" customer experience. This is a noble goal. In their quest, the Ritz-Carlton has implemented a quantitative measurement system to enable the progressive elimination of even the most minute customer service error or problem. You can do this as well in your dental practice.

Ritz-Carlton started by compiling 970 potential problem instances during interaction with customers. They found 1,071 error events! I would expect that just by this exercise alone, Ritz-Carlton is well-positioned to handle any problem, new or old. Every day, in a 15-minute meeting called "The Line-Up," Ritz-Carlton employees review guest experiences, resolve issues, and discuss ways to improve customer service.

3. CORRECTING

In the area of customer service communication, the effort is constant. It extends far beyond a morning huddle or any one meeting into the day-to-day, minute-to-minute workings of your dental office. You may want to employ tiny in-ear headsets for your team to communicate seamlessly throughout the day. With accountability comes empowerment, letting your team members make decisions for immediate service recovery. With results comes shared economics, including awards and a bonus system for jobs well done. Customer service excellence also includes investing in the training and development of team members so they will be able to provide the highest level of customer care possible.

The hard work of customer service is management system correction and perfection. Without management systems to deliver a good product, it does not matter how friendly you are, how nice you are, how beautiful your office is, or how many amenities you have; your patients will leave. Your product includes customer service *and* delivery of excellent dentistry.

Many customer service complaints revolve around breaks in our management systems. Systems need continual update, review, implementation, and improvement. Included in your customer service management system will be reviews of financial performance, product delivery, individual team member performance, service given to the patient, patient experience, patient engagement, patient feedback, team engagement, and teamwork. When all of these aspects are optimized, you will have achieved five-star customer service.

4. COMMUNICATING

The Ritz-Carlton categorizes customer service mishaps into five major categories: Mistakes, Rework, Breakdowns, Inefficiencies, and Variations. They called this system "MR. BIV." This is the Ritz-Carlton's brilliant management system of customer service feedback, correction, and improvement. I love this concept and apply it to dentistry and the dental office management systems. Don't be afraid of MR. BIV! Address MR. BIV and he will go away!

Get organized systematically to log customer service failures so that systems can be continuously implemented and improved. Discuss how MR. BIV can be eliminated from your dental office.

What do you think is the optimal ratio of compliments to criticism when providing constructive comments regarding employee performance? As we get into the hard work of discussing the need for office improvement, let us be reminded of the four to one rule of education. It has been scientifically shown that the optimal ratio of compliments to criticism is four to one. Therefore, as you tackle areas of improvement, give four compliments and get to the point of performance improvement. The usual practice of faint praise followed by harsh criticism ending with faint praise is known by educators as a "sh*tsandwich" that your staff will not be able to digest. Emphasize positive aspects of performance so as to reinforce those behaviors and produce employee reception and openness so that the employee and the team are ready to hear the topic of improvement. The compliments need not be lengthy, but give credit where credit is due before moving on to problem areas.

Examples of compliments could be "Your dress is very professional." "I like the way you greeted the new patient." "It was nice the way you escorted the patient to the chair." "That was great that you provided a warm blanket for the patient. " "Now, we need about one area of improvement."

Mistakes

> *Customers don't expect you to be perfect.*
> *They do expect you to fix things when they go wrong.*
> -Donald Porter

The worst customer service day in our office is when a patient arrives for their appointment and their appliance is not there ready for delivery. This is a HUGE MISTAKE! The patient has been inconvenienced and it is our fault.

Begin by apologizing. We give our patient a gift on the spot. Consider providing a gift card or sending flowers to their home.

Discover which team member did not complete their duty of checking the appliance arrival a day ahead of time. Delivery dates are key in dentistry. The patient may have called and changed their appointment time to a week earlier. The front desk may have missed the change and not informed the lab technician. Another possible reason for missing appliances is lack of lab delivery. Perhaps there is a mailing problem. We expect our appliances to be ready in our office and returned from the lab on or before the due date. We give our patient their next appointment based on an expected appliance or restoration delivery date. Whatever the reason, you need to find the reason for this mistake and devise a new system.

Take corrective action for all mistakes. Review with the team member responsible for checking deliveries for the next day what exactly happened. Was the task of checking omitted? Did carelessness occur? Is it time to reassign this job?

Assign one responsible customer service leader to be accountable to verify all deliveries of appliances and restorations for the next day. Or, schedule the patient after the delivery date when the product has arrived. Have a huddle to discuss the failure to insure that it does not happen again. When you assign a team member this important responsibility and have them accountable, there is still an opportunity to call the patient one day ahead should there be a fabrication or delivery mishap. Should this happen more than once, recheck the return time agreement that you have with your lab or review delivery postal service. You may need to recalculate your turn-around time.

Rework

Rework costs dentists valuable time and money. When the initial impressions are not right, the pour up is poor, or the model broke, make it a team rule to accept nothing less than perfection. Tell the lab to veto poor impressions. Don't accept poor appliances or restorations. Use the best lab possible.

When an impression or scan is not perfect, empower your team members to automatically redo it. If the plaster model breaks, don't glue it back together. Teach your team members to call the patient and have them back for a new impression. This will consistently deliver excellent results.

All of these steps may sound like they would take extra time. I assure you that attempt to salvage with a rework will take you more time as well as reduce the quality of your care. Save yourself from customer service disaster. Maintain a standard of excellence for the highest customer service satisfaction level possible.

Breakdowns

Breakdowns are often secondary to miscommunication. There can be a misunderstanding about the contract, the service, or the office. Be clear about all dental outcomes and experiences. Communicate in writing and with photos whenever possible.

What happens when a patient changes their mind about a long-term treatment like Invisalign on the second tray? Or, perhaps the patient has a removable partial denture made and upon delivery decided that they don't like it. Have clear communication with your patients regarding their contracts and financial obligations. Include that a change in treatment midway, as in the case of choosing braces after choosing Invisalign, will incur further costs.

In the case of Invisalign, have the contract state that the Invisalign down payment, ($2,000 for example), is nonrefundable and nontransferable, whether or not the patient continues with Invisalign. You may state that the orthodontic contract will include $2,000 additional (the down payment for Invisalign) if braces need to go on due to a change of heart regarding Invisalign treatment.

Inefficiencies

> *We cannot afford idleness,*
> *waste or inefficiency.*
> -Eamon de Valera

Inefficiency occurs when there is a break in the chain of events. Steps do not proceed as planned. Time and money is wasted on both the side of the patient, and the side of the office.

Some patients go MIA (missing in action). They miss their appointment and forget to reschedule. We may lose them by not following up right away. Perhaps we attempt to contact them and they do not answer. They are out of sight and out of mind.

When patients do not show up for their appointment, send a text immediately. "No Shows" will usually answer and reschedule. These patients will usually tell you that something came up, they couldn't take time off work, or they just plain forgot. To eliminate "No Shows," it's effective to charge for missed appointments. Consider assessing a small non-refundable down-payment for scheduling long procedure appointments. Tell patients in advance that there will be a charge if canceled without 48-hours' notice.

When I attended the Harvard School of Dental Medicine, I scheduled an appointment with an ophthalmologist. At the initial phone call, the friendly receptionist told me, "If you miss this initial eye exam with the ophthalmologist, there will be a $95 charge." I certainly did not miss this appointment! It was top of mind.

As an orthodontist, if I didn't charge for missed appointments, many of the high school students walking to my office from the high school next door would end up at the corner Burger King with their friends. Indeed, years ago we did not charge for missed appointments, and we found out the hard way that this is what often happened. We added a nominal fee, $35, for a missed appointment. The charge was an immediate flag to parents that their child was not showing up. By adding this small fee, our "No Show" rate quickly went down to almost zero.

If you are still using a paper chart system, don't file the chart of a missing patient. Leave the record in a special area for all cases requiring follow-up. Run your missing patient report daily, weekly, and monthly to continuously monitor for AWOL customers. If you don't hear from them after many contact efforts, perhaps they have moved away. Your attention to patient follow-up will not only remove office inefficiency but also show your current patients how much you value their dental care. Withhold judgement as to why your patient missed their appointments, make every effort to get your dental patient back to the office.

VARIATIONS

Each time the phone rings, the daily office schedule can change. There may be an emergent patient care issue needing to be addressed that day. The mail delivery may be lost, or a product that you have ordered for a procedure may be changed, discontinued, or is out-of-stock. Perturbations in the daily schedule happen constantly, and these variations in office practice will require adaptation and new planning by the team.

Daily, patients call to cancel their appointments, show up early or late, or may show up without even having an appointment. The schedule can be reviewed at the morning huddle, but by the time you get to the noon hour, most likely, the schedule has changed. Communication regarding adjustments needs to be ongoing.

Put the customer first when making schedule change decisions. It is helpful to assign treatment columns or rooms to individual dental assistants. A haphazard "seat the next patient" schedule without individual responsibility leads to chaos. Communicate the change in this assistant's schedule personally to them. An empty appointment in the schedule may be filled by another patient who arrived early, or on a standby call-back list. This will ensure an efficiently- run dental practice with a full schedule.

The Ts

If you can't talk about mistakes you learn nothing.
-Margaret Heffernan

Once you have devoted yourself to management systems for improvement and the four Cs—Collecting, Compiling, Communicating, and Correcting, and addressed MR. BIV—Mistakes, Rework, Breakdowns, Inefficiencies, and Variations, it's time to organize change implementation.

Your Ts are simply areas that need improvement. T can stand for Trouble, a customer service need which needs immediate attention, or it could stand for Thing, as in THE ONE THING. If you focus on one thing and only one thing each day, correcting that area which needs improvement, you may complete hundreds of important tasks over the course of a year.

I once read an insightful book called *The ONE Thing* by Gary Keller and Jay Papasan. Here the authors state that we are often overwhelmed in life by trying to do too many things at the same time. As a result of listing too many tasks, we get nothing done. The authors suggest we concentrate on one task at a time, perhaps one per day—*The ONE Thing*—focus will not be lost and we can be assured of getting at least that one thing done.

It is not possible to fix multiple systems simultaneously, doing it efficiently and well. You may therefore want to start with *The ONE Thing*. Once needed improvements are identified, pick your top Ts each month at your team meeting. Focus on these areas, one at a time. You may want to assign one thing to each team member. Write down your goals of improvement for the month on a whiteboard for all to see. Then, at your next monthly team meeting, review progress and completion of improvement projects.

Let's go over some common *The ONE Thing* examples. Here are a few suggestions for areas of improvement:

> Seating patients on time
> Doctor being on time
> Talking with focus to the patient in front of you
> Being gentle
> Using proper etiquette
> Improving front office/back office communication, hand-off, and patient flow
> Checking appliance on-time delivery/office arrival
> Collect outstanding payments
> Improve new patient exam conversion into start rate
> Check insurance aging and communicating nonpayment to the patient

There will rarely be a time when there is nothing that your office can improve. No outside consultant or management service will be able to let you know what you need to improve as well as your front-line customer service leaders: your dental team. And where will they get their information? It will come directly from their daily office experiences and customer feedback.

I recall one team meeting on August 18, 2011, when we felt that we had nothing in our office that we needed to improve. That was the one and only time this occurred in twenty-seven years of practice! Success was achieved and we celebrated! That feeling lasted for about two days.

Customer service will need constant improvement. Each month, discuss at your team meeting what things, the Ts, or *The ONE Thing* you could improve in the coming month for better, consistent, and smooth customer climate.

The Customer Journey Map

*Empowerment is simple, really.
Give good staff the authority to make a decision and tell
them to use their common sense to improve customer satisfaction.*
-Ron Kaufman

To help improve and prevent customer service breaks, construct a journey map of every customer function. In your dental office, this map would include both on-stage in the reception area and clinical setting, and backstage on the phone and in the lab activities. Each month, mark with a red dot any touchpoints which need improvement due to a mishap or complaint. This exercise will soon reveal your top areas for improvement.

Perhaps there is one individual who is dropping the ball and needs to be placed in a new team role. If your management customer service check points don't work due to a glitch in the human system, the niceties of customer service will be for naught, and you may soon lose the patient. Whatever you find, you can now implement a solution for improved customer service.

Your customers have no knowledge of your management systems, the procedures you supply, or even the equipment you use in your dental office. Your patients want a functional, esthetic, and comfortable dental product to serve their needs. Your customers will only remember whether or not they enjoyed their experience in your office. In an enjoyable climate, people connect with people and the experience, rather than management systems, which should run smoothly and effortlessly in the background, sight unseen.

Build Confidence

*With confidence,
you have won before you have started.*
-Marcus Garvey

As you build empowerment of your customer service leaders, don't forget to celebrate your success along the way. Acknowledge and reward efforts and victories. Mentor service leaders and encourage them with praise for a job well done.

If a customer service leader brings a situation to the dentist which they should handle themselves, mentor them to address the situation through to completion. If they make a good decision, acknowledge them and give public praise. Doing so promotes empowerment, engagement, and confidence. Empowering your team is a win-win decision for everyone.

Chapter 15

PREPAREDNESS

Never forget, with every new employee and every new customer you have only one chance... just one, to make a great first impression.
-Mac Anderson

"Wow. This place feels fantastic!" From the moment you walk through the door, you feel positive energy, you hear happy laughter, and you see more smiles than usual. This place not only looks fabulous, it smells great, and it may even elicit happy memories. There are beautiful items to be seen. There may be soft items to touch. There are yummy treats to eat. Inviting, friendly, happy, smiling people are all around. Their contentment is projected to you. You say to yourself, "I love it here!"

Think of your favorite customer service experience. What superstar place would it be? The Four Seasons? Nordstrom's? A health spa? Imagine it for a minute. How does it look, smell, sound, taste, and feel? What does it do to elicit positive responses from your five senses? Could this place be your dental office?

THE FIVE SENSES

The three senses: sight, hearing, and smell cannot well be prevented; touch and taste not at all.
-Leonardo da Vinci

1. SIGHT

Sight is a function of the eyes but vision is a function of the heart.
-Marcus Garvey

The first person that a new patient and their family talks to or sees is your most important customer service leader. They will create an impression of your office within the first seven seconds of entry. This concierge must be welcoming, approachable, friendly, helpful, and enthusiastic. They must look and act professional. They must relay immediately your office culture, care, and climate. This person must be engaged in the vital job that they have been given.

The office greeter will provide a new patient with the first impression of your office. In a five-star hotel, outstanding customer service starts with a great concierge. Whoever sits closest to the door of entry must be prepared to conscientiously be the new patient ambassador. This person is prepared to warmly welcome the new patient/family as well as attend to their every need. The office concierge is your office hostess. She welcomes patients as you would welcome friends and families to your home. She makes everyone in the reception area comfortable. She sets the tone for the patient experience.

Have your customer service leaders approach each patient as if they were entertaining at a fancy resort, cruise ship, or "Fantasy Island." They need to be escorted to each step along the way. Stand and give new customers a warm welcome. Offer them refreshment. Give them an office tour and be sure that each team member greets them enthusiastically with a smile. The doctor should reassure each patient and family member that they have come to the right place, their personal dental utopia!

The office concierge should prepare a daily roster of new patients. A personalized welcome folder of informational materials should be readied. The front desk concierge should oversee patient flow so as to keep the appointment on time. Remember, the new patient appointment is the highest priority for the dental office. The concierge will need to alert the team that "It's Showtime" for the new arrival.

Consultants often state that there is a treatment area versus front office tug for the doctor's attention. Priority needs to be given to the new patient exam. The assistant, after briefing the doctor about the new patient and having the doctor review the medical history, will guide the doctor into the exam room. The doctor may be attracted to many other activities in the office. Focus is best placed on the new patient.

CLEANLINESS

> *Cleanliness is indeed next to godliness.*
> -Christopher Morley

Someone once asked Michael Eisner, CEO of Disney, "What is your number one job?"

Mr. Eisner answered, "To pick up trash!" That's a pretty remarkable answer from a guy who earns $50,000,000 per year!

You may be a fabulous doctor with a wonderful team that delivers outstanding dentistry, but if your office is not clean, your patients may end up choosing treatment elsewhere. First impressions count, especially when it comes to healthcare. Your cleanliness speaks to your clinical excellence. Your dental office must be meticulously, immaculately clean.

To accomplish office clean-up, appoint an Office Cleanliness Coordinator (OCC). The OCC will manage maintenance items such as: immediate repair of broken items, removal of stains, repair of rips, vacuuming, cleaning, polishing, and organization of all clean-up office projects. She will also clean the mirrors at brushing stations and sinks throughout the day to keep them spot-free. A visit to the public bathroom during the work day is also a good idea to make sure tissues are well-stocked and visitors haven't been too messy.

Think of Walt Disney World. Someone is always cleaning. At Disney World, there is not a speck of litter on the ground. If a gum wrapper has fallen, a customer service leader, no matter who it is—CEO or maintenance crew—will immediately pick it up. It is the same for you in your dental office. Every team member has the responsibility of cleanliness. This holds true especially for the doctor, often the messiest person of all.

Countertops must be clean and as paper-free as possible. This is especially important in the digital age when patients may be taking photos in your office. Guard that no patient names are ever visible as it is a violation of HIPAA. You may want to restrict photos to one designated zone.

Consider hiring a local professional cleaning service. The cost is well worth it. They will clean your restrooms and empty your trash daily. They can water plants, wash windows, polish surfaces, and sweep the floors. On an annual bases, they can deep clean carpets and shine hardwood or tile flooring.

BUILDING EXTERIOR
Cheerful yellow African daisies greet patients as they walk to the front door of Deer Valley Dental Professionals at 5201 Deer Valley Road in Antioch, California. The bushes are trimmed and sidewalks are swept. Parking lot lines are freshly-painted and there is a handicapped ramp for older patients. The front door handles are newly replaced and in excellent condition. Examine your exterior grounds. What emotional response does your entryway create?

Start by taking a walk around your parking lot. Pick up any papers, napkins, cigarette butts, aluminum cans, and anything else you can find that would negatively impact your brand, and your customer service experience. The first impression of your dental office and dental treatment begins in the parking lot. Even if you are a renter and have a groundskeeper, be sure that your parking area is clean, well-lit, and safe.

Adequate lighting is vital for safety. Customer needs include disabled parking spaces painted in bright colors and wheelchair ramps, and other necessary accommodations under the Americans with Disabilities Act. By requiring team members to park far from the front door, you offer the best and closest parking for your patients. You may even want to place a special sign closest to your front door reading, "Reserved for the new dental patient of Dr. YZ."

Wayfinding is another important consideration. In a larger building, would a new family be able to easily and quickly locate your office? Is the signage clear? Are directions easy to understand? Make sure you pay attention to such "navigational" tools not only for patient ease of service but also for marketing.

I once visited a major medical center to meet with an oral surgeon with whom I was working on an orthognathic surgical case. It was difficult for me to find the office because I did not know it would be listed as Maxillofacial Oral Surgery rather than Oral Surgery in the hospital directory. Another time, I visited a dentist in a major medical center who had an office on the third floor. There was no signage at the entrance. I asked the concierge where the dental office was and was directed to the third floor. When I got off the elevator there was no directory. I finally found the office. The lack of signage was not helping patients or building the practice.

It's so nice when the grocery bagger at the grocery store asks, "Do you need assistance to your car?" You can do the same for your dental patients. Offer to have someone walk the patient to their car after a long procedure. Escort elderly patients whenever possible.

Take another moment and walk into your office through your front door. If your front door is not in excellent condition, and free of scratches, paint chips, and fingerprints, customers may assume that the rest of your office may be the same. The building entrance must be inviting. Receptacles for landfill, compost, and recyclable waste should be tastefully placed but readily accessible.

RECEPTION AREA

As you enter Tiffany's you notice that the displays and countertops glitter. Everything is pristine. The surfaces you see shine. Whether glass, metal, or wood, the surfaces are being continuously polished. Tremendous effort is given to making every surface pleasing to the eye. Do the same in your dental office. Make it a priority to dust and use surface cleaner throughout the day. Vacuum daily. Go for the five-star look!

Occasionally, have an outside inspector, perhaps an interior design consultant, come to do a "white glove" walk-through at your dental office. Let this person create a "To Do" list of maintenance items that they identify. Find and correct scratches, chips, stains, and imperfections. Eliminate clutter. Shipping boxes and mail should be out of sight or neatly stored away from the traffic flow of patient care and customer service scheduling at the front desk. Simplify for a pleasing visual experience.

Restock magazines weekly. Consider taking a poll and asking your patients what magazines they like most and then supplying those magazines in your reception area. Magazines need to be tidy, in good condition, and not overflowing. Check your new magazines each week and keep current, interesting, beautiful, and G-rated magazines for display. Remove magazines with negative, uninviting headlines. Magazines will be left throughout the office. Have a lunchtime and end-of-day magazine clean-up.

Consider having some reception area visual entertainment. Patients love watching current events. Sports events like World Cup or the Olympics are always popular. When sports are playing on our reception room TV, sometimes the patients want to keep watching when it is time for their appointment.

Movies can no longer be publicly played in the reception area without purchase of an annual movie license. The movie industry contacted me after seeing a picture of Mater from the movie *Cars II* in an office tour video posted on YouTube. Amazing that they could find this and that it was worth their time to contact me for an annual movie license costing about $850 per year. You would think that the movie industry would be happy that you are buying their movies and playing them in your reception room. We now play cable television and the patients and their families love it.

TREATMENT AREAS

Concentrate on those office areas within a patient's normal visual field. This would include all countertops. All surfaces should be clutter free. The quality and care of the office chairs must always be maintained. Reupholster when rips or stains appear. Lights need to be continually checked for burned out bulbs. Wall paper, walls, and carpets must be continually maintained.

Patients are looking at every detail, especially when they are brushing their teeth or in the dental chair staring at the walls or ceiling. Make sure that there are no water spots, cracks, dust, or cobwebs. Patients will also look down at the floor. Be sure carpets are clean and that tiles are not chipped.

Try dividing office maintenance into areas assigned to each staff member. Preparedness will then become a team effort, and every customer service leader will be engaged in the important job of keeping the office in tip-top shape.

RESTROOMS

Cleanliness matters. In his book, *212 Degree Service*, Mac Andersen describes a research study of the Ritz-Carlton which asked about service, accommodations, and ambience. The study revealed that guests did not care about the exquisite green marble imported from Italy in their bathrooms. Customers preferred that their bathroom be pure white so that they could see that it was clean. It is the same for you in your dental office.

Don't expect the cleaning service that visits the building every evening to do it—keep restrooms clean throughout the day. By the time you get a restroom complaint, it's too late! Check the public restroom several times per day. Make a schedule, such as 11:00 a.m., 1:00 p.m., 3:00 p.m., and 4:30 p.m. for restroom checks. After-school kids can be brutal to restrooms.

Even your restroom reflects the quality of your work, how much you value your patients and employees, and the quality of service you provide. Keep your patient restroom squeaky clean, and your office will be a pleasure to visit.

STERILIZATION

The new patient's decision may be influenced by their perception of how clean your office is and the excellence of your sterilization. Take a moment to emphasize that all instruments are scrubbed, cleaned, bagged, and sterilized to the highest standards in the dental industry during your new patient office tour.

Cleanliness is Everyone's Responsibility
Patti, DA, Office Maintenance Coordinator

"I have a very important job, office cleanliness. Patients must never see a dirty, untidy office or experience equipment maintenance problems. Office preparedness is everyone's responsibility. It needs continuous time and attention. This is an important aspect of teamwork since no one should leave a mess or dirty instruments for someone else on the team to clean.

"Sometimes the doctor may need cleanliness training. The doctor's desk is always a challenge. Having a special office clean-up day gives everyone in the office a chance to get organized, get caught up, and get cleaned up. This is especially true for the doctor.

"The doctor may also need reminding to never touch things in the office while wearing gloves. Gloves must be removed and left on the treatment tray whenever the doctor stands. Otherwise, assistants trail the doctor, cleaning everything and reminding the doctor of OSHA standards.

"I love working in the orthodontic office and working in dentistry. My job duties also include sterilization, lab duties, and overlay retainer and mouthguard fabrication. In my free time out of the office, I also work in the private cleaning profession. The title of Dental Assistant, Office Maintenance Coordinator is perfect for me!"

2. SOUND

> *Remember that a person's name is to that person*
> *the sweetest and most important sound in any language.*
> -Dale Carnegie

"Mr. Bond, Mr. James Bond?" Calling someone by name is music to their ears. Make your patients feel like James Bond or Vespa, the real life World War II Polish spy about whom Ian Fleming wrote the James Bond novels.

What patients hear is important. Preparedness includes the words and phrases that you use. Saying hello, using the patient's name, thanking each patient, and giving a fond farewell are fundamental. Make your patient's visit personalized and memorable through conversation. Your greeting starts the patient experience. Small talk and laughter make the experience fun. Your thank you warms the patient's heart and leaves them with a lasting impression of your dental office. Your fond farewell welcomes the patient back for another appointment and will be the last memory your patient holds in their mind until they return.

Music soothes the savage beast. Music also induces added comfort to a dental patient. Cool jazz is relaxing. Spa music puts patients at ease. Soft rock may bring back high school memories in the older set. Pop rock appeals to the young patients and energizes the team. You want the sounds of your office to be what patients want to hear. To accomplish this, play music without commercials. Try Sirius XM satellite radio. Pay attention to the volume, keeping it at a pleasing level.

A flat screen TV playing softly within your reception area contributes to patient calmness and enjoyment. The day I installed a flat screen TV in my reception area, patients and their families sat for the first time with a new calmness enthralled in what was on the set. Our reception room went from a high activity, constant motion environment with loud conversation to an atmosphere of quiet entertainment and relaxation. There were no more questions at the front desk such as, "What time is my appointment?" The reception area became a place of added comfort and joy.

3. SCENT

Nothing is more memorable than a smell.
One scent can be unexpected, momentary and fleeting,
yet conjure up a childhood summer beside a lake in the mountains.
-Diane Ackerman

Smell is closely linked to memory. Much of what we smell takes us back to an earlier happy time in life, baking chocolate chip cookies with Mom or burning Christmas candles at home. Wouldn't it be great if our dental office smelled like the ocean reminding us of a special family vacation? Whether it be home, a resort, or a dental office, often the first impression that we have of a place is its smell. Let aroma help your dental office make that initial impression great.

One dental office in our community won our aromatherapy customer service award. Upon entering this office, it smelled absolutely delicious! This exceptional office definitely achieved five-star "Spa" level aroma excellence! I asked the dentist what was his aroma secret. He stated that in the treatment area, he had a lamp that warmed aroma wax. He showed me an attractive vase-like object with a light heating a puddle of fragrant wax. Taking in the delicious scent, all I could say was, "Wow!" Aromatherapy definitely adds a special sensory feeling of nostalgia, ease, and comfort.

At the Main Street entrance of Disneyland Magic Kingdom, there is a candy shop. There, candy makers make peanut brittle in a special room behind observation windows that allow all visitors to watch through the glass. Special ventilators push this delicious aroma out to Main Street. A Disneyland guest can smell the peanut brittle of the candy room from the entrance one block away. This subliminal scent makes every Disneyland guest say, "I love this place!" Once the aroma fan was installed, peanut brittle sales quadrupled on Main Street, Disneyland.

I love it when a patient tells me, "Your office smells great!" We usually get this response when we burn an aroma candle with a delicious fragrance such as vanilla. In the fall, when the Keurig coffee maker is getting frequent use, we often smell a hint of pumpkin spice. It gives us all a cozy family feeling of home, even when at the orthodontic office.

Scent is crucial to your office success. Does your dentistry smell delicious? Does your office scent emote a happy memory? It is possible to become immune to your own office smell. Ask friends occasionally how your office smells. Clean (but not antiseptic) and inviting are great office scents for optimal branding.

Like Disneyland, the best offices use aromatherapy to their advantage. Our office makes occasional gift delivery visits to our referring offices. We visit over 100 offices annually, often visiting as many as fifteen offices in a single day. Exceptional customer service five-star dental offices smell great. Most offices smell fine. But some dental offices smell really badly. Whether it be from mold, mildew, discarded food, or old carpeting, these dental offices would benefit tremendously from a "refresher" course.

Our favorite fragrance brand at Gorczyca Orthodontics is Hawaiian Tropic Breeze by Glade. We burn Hawaiian Tropic Breeze aromatic candles and utilize Hawaiian Tropic Breeze aerosols. Hawaii and Alaska are, after all, the two happiest states in the US. If our office smells great and reminds our visitors of Hawaii, how can our patients be anything but happy to see us? Scented hand wash also perfuses aroma throughout the clinical area.

There are two wonderful things that customers will enjoy smelling. One is a fragrance. Consider placing aroma sticks, a Glade Plug-In, candles, wax votives, or other fragrance dispensers in your treatment areas. The second thing that customers enjoy smelling is food, which the patient could eat. Fresh baked cookies and other baked goods smell great and are welcomed in the refreshment area. Vanilla and cinnamon are delicious fragrances and enjoyable to be around.

LUNCH FOOD

While on the subject of scent, remember that our lunch food is a destroyer of office freshness and customer service excellence. Beware of placing food waste in garbage cans near patient reception. If your team eats lunch in your dental office, be sure that garbage cans used for clean-up are far away from patient areas. Tie and remove lunch garbage. To prevent reception room smell, drinks other than coffee or water should never be brought to the front desk. Food should never be present at the front desk.

4. TOUCH

Feelings aroused by the touch of someone's hand,
the sound of music, the smell of a flower,
a beautiful sunset, a work of art,
love, laughter, hope and faith—
all work on the unconscious and the conscious aspects of the self,
and they have physiological consequences as well.
-Bernie Siegel

Never underestimate human touch. Touch can relay caring, comfort, and gentleness. It will put your patients at ease, whether it be a handshake, hug, or soft hand on the shoulder as you lay the patient back in the treatment chair.

Your handshake will be the first "touch" for the new patient. It conveys, "Welcome. We're happy to see you today," "You are important to us," and "We're glad that you are here." A strong handshake grip expresses confidence and control. "We'll take great care of you" is immediately conveyed. A limp handshake conveys reluctance or lack of confidence. The new patient may think, *Are you new around here? Do you know what you are doing?* No handshake at all eliminates the connection between two people. It conveys a cold environment. The new patient may question, *Do you even care?*

Be mindful of touch items in your office. Soft items release tension, especially in children. Beanie Babies, Pillow Pets, or a soft comfort blanket are all items that can improve the patient mood and experience. Therapy dogs can also be found in some dental offices. Even a stuffed animal when hugged can relieve stress and put a smile on children's faces. Make a soft comfort mascot a member of your dental team.

THE DENTAL SPA

Dr. Anissa Holmes of Jamaica Cosmetic Dental Services and her amazing team give hand massages to their patients during their appointment. Pillows, blankets, hand massages, or warm gloves certainly produce relaxation and comfort. These feelings of wellbeing help to eliminate fear. Now the dental office appointment becomes a total body experience.

Serve the whole patient in a holistic way. Every dental touchpoint is an opportunity to offer amazing customer service through extended services. Here dental treatment enters the realm of hospitality.

Ask your patient if they would like a soft blanket for their long procedure or warm hand glove. Perhaps they would like to remove their shoes. Try giving your patient a lavender neck comforter. Touching something soft during a dental procedure can be extremely comforting.

TEMPERATURE

Cool temperatures feel good especially on a hot day in California. Cool temperatures are also great climates to work in. Air conditioning and cool room temperature gives you the opportunity to offer your patient a warm cozy blanket.

Have you ever felt the bath robe, towels, or comforter in a five-star resort? Putting on one of these soft, luxurious coverings is a memorable experience. It can be the same for your patients in your dental office. Let your patients kick off their shoes and snuggle up for their dental procedure.

Warm temperatures make patients feel uneasy or anxious. The patient may start to sweat even before the start of any dental procedure. The patient may want to leave. This is especially important to realize in hot climates. Even if you need a portable fan, be sure your patient stays cool and comfortable during the dental procedure.

5. TASTE

Starbucks has a bold and meaningful relationship with people that is not only about the coffee.
-Howard Schultz

Edible experiences are beyond comparison. A company called Intentional Chocolate performed a blind study at the University of Wisconsin in which the researchers tested the well-being of consumers after tasting their chocolate product. The Intentional Chocolate improved the overall mood of consumers by more than sixty-seven percent!

While writing this book, I attended my son's music camp at the Philadelphia International Music Festival held at Bryn Mawr College. There, I asked my son's floor master, "What's the most memorable thing about your daughter's orthodontist?"

The floor master couldn't wait to tell me his reply. "When my daughter had her Phase I orthodontic exam, after the exam was over, the front desk receptionist gave my daughter a chocolate chip cookie. It was a fresh baked cookie in a little white paper bag. My daughter couldn't wait to go back to this office to get another cookie!"

One of my greatest joys at Gorczyca Orthodontics is giving patients and their families a small chocolate treat during the Valentine's season. This gesture makes patients so happy! For a really special over-the-top treat, we have a chocolate fountain. Although messy, chocolate with fresh fruit for dipping definitely produces the Wow! factor. This event produces great word-of-mouth internal marketing, and it keeps patients wanting to come back. Try it and see!

A study done by a restaurant group found that polite restaurant service will get a tip. Polite service with a chocolate gave a seventeen percent increase in service tips. Polite service with chocolate and then asking would anyone like more chocolate led to a twenty-four percent tip increase. Put a little chocolate in your dental office.

Almost everyone loves coffee or tea. A fresh cup of coffee in the morning for a busy mom is like a mini vacation. Don't lose out on this customer service opportunity to be one of the most wonderful gathering places in your office complex. Serving refreshments with coffee is one of your greatest customer service opportunities. Small cinnamon rolls or biscotti create a taste experience.

Give your patients something to taste at your office other than acid etch, bonding adhesive, or mouthwash. Offer coffee, tea, juice, or cucumber spa water. Put a little thought and attention into office taste. Make your dental office a tasteful, yummy place to be!

YOUR OFFICE SCHEDULE

*They key is not to prioritize what's on your schedule,
but to schedule your priorities.*
-Stephen Covey

For maximum comfort to your patients, do not over schedule ever. When the office is overscheduled, everyone loses. It is not an excellent problem to have—it will ultimately decrease revenue from disgruntled patients. An overcrowded office makes patients feel unvalued. Patients assume that the office is messy due to the high volume of patients or that the office does not want additional new patients. Being overcrowded also makes it impossible for your patients to bring family and friends to appointments. It's hard to be comfortable in a crowd. Make patient comfort and ease part of your concierge service.

To best seat patients on time, have an overflow chair. Get patients seated on time. The Clinic Coordinator needs to keep the flow of patient care going, directing the doctor to where to go next. When all chairs are filled, the team members can lightly tap on the doctor's shoulder as a silent sign to indicate that it's time to wrap up the small talk and move on to the next patient, so as to stay on schedule.

WHEN THE FEELING'S RIGHT

> *Your customer doesn't care how much you know until they know how much you care.*
> -Damon Richards

Customers feel with their hearts and their minds with input from the five senses. In preparing your office experience, consider these five senses of perception. What do patients see? What do they hear? What do they smell? What do they touch? What do they taste? Bringing it all together—sight, sound, smell, touch, taste,—is the sum total of what your patients experience.

It is your customer service goal to have every patient feel great before, during, and especially after their dental procedure. Give your patients a comfort break. Listen to them. When the feeling's right, patients will eagerly return to your office for a lifetime of dental care.

Chapter 16

ASSISTANCE

A customer is four times more likely to buy from a competitor if the problem is service related vs. product or price related.
-Bain & Company

Dental patients need constant attention, reassurance, and help. Whether it is coordinating their next cleaning, scheduling an appointment, or finding an oral surgeon for third molar extraction, every offer of assistance is a reassurance that they have made the right decision in choosing your office for their dental health.

"I'll help you." The dental office which learns these three words will quickly become known for excellent customer service. Entire books have been written about polite phrases and service language. Scripts can be practiced. Phrases can be learned. Scenes can be memorized.

In the movie *My Fair Lady*, a British shop girl is turned into a high-fashion lady of society with a little help of a caring professor who improves her language and dresses her up. It can be the same in your dental office, as you practice polite phrases with team members who are a little "rough around the edges," dress them up to look professional, and groom them to become customer service leaders.

I was once in a hotel café in Carmel, California, where a very fine waiter who spoke English as a second language impressed me with his courteous, polite speech and etiquette. His service was impeccable. As he was a newcomer to the US, I asked him how he had learned the

English language so well in such a short period of time. He told me that he had married a woman originally from Germany who also had English as her second language. Together, they had worked on their language skills, every day, repeating phrases and memorizing the rules of grammar. This left a big impression on me that everyone in the dental office could and should be able to improve their English language skills in the same way for the benefit of the patients whom we serve. We can all sound professional in our effort to deliver outstanding customer service.

Little things add up. Like a bellman in a five-star hotel asking, "May I take your bags to your room?" you may do the same by asking a patient who has just had a long dental procedure, "May I walk you to your car?"

Think of "little" things you can do for your customers. They surprise and delight. They make you remarkable. They build your company brand.

Assistance is service at the highest level. It's doing extra things for the customer. It's going the extra mile. Never underestimate the value of offering assistance.

Assistance comes in many forms. These include being friendly, supportive, positive, precise, and timely. Choose the assistance style that is right for you and the members of your team. Let's go through a few examples.

Five Characteristics of Assistance

> *We believe that customer service shouldn't just be a department.*
> *It should be the entire company.*
> -Tony Hsieh

1. FRIENDLY

"Please allow me to help you."

Like an airline stewardess on a transcontinental flight, your customer service leaders are there to assist the patient whenever they can, with whatever they can do, in a friendly manner. Whether it is assistance with scheduling their dental appointments in your office and other offices, escorting the patient from place to place, or explaining services, the words, "Please allow me to assist you" need to be spoken as much as possible, with a smile on the dental assistant's face.

To offer friendly assistance, you must truly know your customer. Friendliness will require patience and listening. No matter how trivial or repetitive your patient service request may be, like a good friend, you need to maintain a cool and caring demeanor, being there for your patient even if service is running into your lunchtime or after hours. Take time to listen and don't rush. Reassure your patient that it is your pleasure to help them, and that you will always be there for them. A friend is never a burden.

2. SUPPORTIVE

"What questions do you have for me?"

Read your patient's emotional state when you are offering assistance. Evaluate their mood, level of patience, and personality. You don't want to misread a patient as being in a hurry when they are not. Don't confuse a patient who is looking to spend more time in your office and have more questions answered with one who is in a hurry to leave the office.

Asking more questions is a good customer service tool. It will allow the patient to either ask more questions or tell you, "You've answered all my questions. You've done a great job. I am completely satisfied. I'm now happy to start treatment in your office."

Take time to follow-up with your patients. This may sometimes require an evening phone call to ask how your patient is doing. Customers want to know that their thoughts and feelings matter. By listening, you express empathy. Questions show that you care, strengthening the good relationship you share with your patient.

3. POSITIVE

"It is my pleasure to assist you."

To offer your customers the assistance that they desire, you are going to need to "read" them, anticipate what is causing them distress, and offer assistance. Let me give you an example.

For instance, imagine that a patient doesn't get their follow through with the specialty dental procedure that you have recommended. This is a customer service opportunity. Escort the patient to the front desk, offer to call the specialty dental office for them, and ask if the appointment could be facilitated so that the patient could be seen today. the patient will be very pleased that you took corrective action to promptly get them in to see your colleague, whether the general dentist or a specialist.

Often in dentistry, assistance means making decisions and scheduling the necessary next steps for the patient. Patients are looking for guidance. By facilitating and helping to execute their referrals, you are providing your patient with great customer service and showing them that you have their best interests at heart. This will enable you to provide your patients with excellent dental care. Assess the customer's emotional state and assist. Focus your attention outward.

4. PRECISE

"Let me show you a model of your proposed treatment."

Your diagnosis and treatment plan need to be precise in the solutions provided to the patient. Deliver what you promise. Help the dental patient fulfill their treatment plan by helping them adhere to the care plan and by keeping treatment affordable.

Case acceptance improves drastically when the patient can see the final result that is expected. Never underestimate the assistance of a diagnostic wax-up in assisting your patient to make a treatment decision. For a partially edentulous patient or a patient coordinating orthodontic treatment with multiple implants and restorative treatment including veneers, a diagnostic wax-up communicates a life-changing result. It is a valuable tool of communication not only with the patient but also with all doctors on the interdisciplinary team.

5. TIMELY

"Let's schedule all of your appointments today so that this treatment can be completed as quickly as possible."

Solve patient's problems before they start. Outline the steps of treatment and write them down for the patient. Make phone calls to specialists and appointments for the patient. With proactive, timely support, the treatment gets done in the shortest time possible. Here the desires and specifications of the patient in their care process are fulfilled.

Timely treatment is most important when the patient is planning their wedding. The patient wants their teeth straight and their veneers done, and they need it done quickly. Often the orthodontist and general dentist will not have much time, maybe six months or less, to give the patient the smile of their dreams for their wedding day. Offer to schedule all the appointments on the first day to fulfill the patient's timely request and needs.

In the special case of weddings, consider, after the treatment is planned and accepted, starting the day of the exam. Stay late. If you are an orthodontist, put the braces on that day and get started. Having all the wire change appointments scheduled with the debond appointment and completion date set will be excellent customer service and tells the patient that they will get the care they desire to be ready for their special day. Call the restorative dentist and schedule the veneers prep appointment that day for a future date. The patient will be delighted, and they will know that they made a smart choice in their dental care provider.

Welcome to Our Office. We're Happy You're Here
Pam, Patient Coordinator, Front Desk Concierge

"As patient concierge at the front desk, I am thrilled to welcome our new patients and all patients. I love my job at the front desk. Every day is a new adventure in customer service. When you visit our office, you will find a positive and energy-filled environment. We love our patients and it shows.

"When you enter our office, you will immediately see our happy and devoted team members. Our professional portraits are displayed by name on the front reception area wall which we call 'Our Team Wall of Fame'. Included here is our mission statement: Caring professionals serving valued patients. This is what each of our team members aims to be. Service is what we aim to deliver.

"We have three service goal core values: clinical excellence, outstanding customer service, and a great patient experience. I am happy to be part of the start of every new patient experience.

"Every patient has my promise that I will make their care in our office as enjoyable and easy as possible. I give each patient my appreciation and fond farewell with thanks for choosing our office and referring their family and friends. Each day I tell our patients that I look forward to seeing them again soon."

Be appreciative of the opportunity your patient has given you to provide them service and assistance. When the patient's treatment is over, offer them a thank you perhaps in the form of a patient referral gift card or a small token of appreciation. It is a pleasure and a privilege to assist patients on their journey to dental health.

Chapter 17

FULFILLMENT

*Never try to fit your customers into
what you think they want.
Ask them, and they will tell you.*
                         -Tom Pickett

It is our job as part of the service industry of dentistry to fulfill our patient's needs and desires. In achieving excellence in fulfillment, the greatest resource we have is the feedback of our customers. Great customer service is a state of constant asking and listening. Here are six ways to listen so that you gain customer feedback and achieve customer fulfillment.

SIX FORMS OF CUSTOMER FEEDBACK

*We all need people who give us feedback.
That's how we improve.*
                         -Bill Gates

1. ASK

These four simple words, "How were things today?" are very powerful. Listen to your patients carefully and keep your patients in your communication loop. The doctor and patient circles of communication should actually be intersecting Venn diagrams. This is the foundation of your word-of-mouth internal marketing.

Keep a record of patient responses, delivering a report so that suggestions for improvement can be made at each monthly team meeting. To assess customer fulfillment, be sure to ask these four simple words.

2. POSTCARD SURVEY

A quick, informal, "Tell Us What You Think" check-the-box survey at the coffee counter is a great way to get fast feedback. Make this a postal card by adding your office name and address to the reverse side. This will enable your patients to send you anonymous feedback. This card could have just three questions:

1. Please grade our customer service 5–1 stars.
2. What do you like about our office?
3. What could we do better?

By making your queries open-ended, you will let them tell you what they think. You will get many creative ideas about making your office remarkable and even more customer friendly. Your patient may have responded, "I'd love a biscotti with my coffee." Give it to them. It's fine as long as they don't have braces!

3. A FORMAL SURVEY

Posted on your website or handed to patients, your survey should be readily available for immediate feedback. This survey will include many aspects of your office service in addition to listing the name of each team member and the doctor for individual service comments. Keep the survey as short as possible. For a written survey handed to the patient, make it two pages maximum. Review the results of the survey at each monthly team meeting. File individual employee comments for review at annual performance appraisals.

Suggested questions might be, "How satisfied are you with your customer experience in our office?" "What could we do better?" or "How likely are you to refer your family and friends?"

An open-ended question, "What improvements can we make to our office?" might take too much time and be left blank. If it is answered, it will give you valuable information. Ways to answer could include a grading system, 1-10, 10 being excellent and 1 being poor. In this way, your office and individual team members, as well as the doctor, can keep track of these scores in a continuous effort to improve. This applies to certain questions, not open-ended ones.

Instead of open or 1 through 10, Press-Ganey survey of medical doctors uses five categories of answers ranging from "Never" to "Always." "Always" is considered the top box score. Your survey may ask questions like, "Was the doctor skillful and gentle in all areas of her task?" This is a Yes-No question and not as effective for feedback.

Evaluate your metric. At many medical centers, doctors and staff must aim for greater than ninety percent of patient satisfaction surveys being returned with "top box" scores. By getting your customer responses, you will be able to make improvements to your office and rework things for the maximum benefit and delight of your patients.

Without a questionnaire, there will be things that your customers desire that you will not know about. If you sense that a customer has something that they would like to tell you, hand them the questionnaire. It is much better to have patients air their thoughts and feelings on your questionnaire than to have them write anything negative on a social media site.

4. VIP FEEDBACK

Identify your most valued and trusted customers. These are your adoring fans and top referrers. They serve as practice ambassadors. Keep them in your mind and in your heart. Stay in touch. Make them part of your virtual team. Ask them what you could improve and get it done. Ask them what they like most about your service. Invite them to participate in video testimonials or to give a five-star review on Yelp. Do more of that.

5. CALL PATIENTS WHO DID NOT START TREATMENT

It's valuable customer service feedback to follow-up with your non-start patients. Ask, "What can we do to get you started?" The doctor can and should personally make this call. It is a great source of consumer feedback. This is applicable to all patients and all dental procedures.

At Gorczyca Orthodontics, non-start hurdles are usually financial. This is a great opportunity to offer outside financing of equal payments spanning over five years. Yet, some patients cannot afford the monthly payments. Everything is negotiable. It's up to your office to decide what is possible to facilitate treatment.

6. ASK YOUR TEAM MEMBERS

Let's not forget the direct office feedback from your dental team. Ask often and ask frequently. Start your quest for improvements with those who know your office best. Ask, "If there is one thing that you could change about the office, what would it be?" Your team members are the best consultants you will ever find. They also have the most interaction with customers at every touchpoint in the office. Ask your team what improvements each individual could make.

Your Guarantee

*Making a sale makes money,
keeping a customer makes a lot of money.*
-Dr. Michael Le Boeuf

You know your patients will be fulfilled when you guarantee satisfaction. The last thing a dentist ever wants is a patient who is dissatisfied with treatment or the delivery of treatment. Whether it be orthodontics, restorative dentistry, or any other type of dental care, the final result matters. It is paramount to continue to do your best to serve the patient until treatment is right for them. Occasionally, this will include redoing a treatment, sending something back to the lab undelivered, retaking impressions or a scan, or revising a diagnostic wax-up. Making this extra effort may mean the difference between keeping or losing a patient.

One way to guarantee satisfaction in orthodontics is to have a debond request agreement. This final document simply states, "I have been told that my orthodontic treatment is complete. I am happy and satisfied with the result and I am requesting the removal of my braces." It also states, "I understand that I will need to wear my retainers to maintain this result."

A debond letter has many valuable functions. Should the patient not wear their retainer, it prevents them from saying, "I think you took the braces off too soon," or "I wasn't completely satisfied." Take final records also on every patient. Although the patient is not an expert dental professional, this letter and final records do serve as documentation of patient satisfaction and the excellent result delivered.

A final treatment letter also serves as a document that the patient is aware of their final payment if estimated insurance payment has not yet been collected—this final amount owed figure will appear. Like an initial contract, a final contract insures and documents that all parties are in agreement with the financial obligations at the completion of treatment and that the patient understands that the estimated insurance payment may not be collected in full and that they have a final financial obligation to the office.

For the dentists who treat patients in this way, patient expectations will be exceeded. Eventually your patient will become an evangelist for your dental practice.

Ten-Year Retainer Checks

As an orthodontist, nothing makes us happier than to see our patients ten years later with a beautiful, stable occlusion and wonderful smile. Let your patients know that they are patients for life. Invite them back for a complimentary ten-year retainer check. This is a great way to reconnect with your patients and also to meet their children and maybe even grandchildren. Let your patients know that your relationship doesn't end the day their braces come off or their contract ends. As their dental healthcare provider, you will always be there for them, at their service.

Assessing Happiness

> *There is only one happiness in this life,*
> *to love and be loved.*
> -George Sand

As you give your dental patient a fond farewell at the end of each appointment, take time to assess their level of happiness with their dental achievements. You may find that once one dental service is completed, other unexpected needs and requests arise. For example, once orthodontics is completed and teeth look straight, the need to replace old crowns appears. Continue to fulfill your patient's dental needs and wants by asking questions about how they feel about their teeth.

Realize that your job as a dentist will never truly be done. When your patients make dental health a priority, they will continue to strive for dental health excellence. The more educated your patients become, the more focused they are on dental solutions.

Praise your patients for their investment in oral health. Dentistry increases confidence and changes lives. Remind your patients of the tremendous progress they have made with their dental health. Tell them how much you love seeing their new smile. Give your dental patients the gift of dental happiness and fulfillment!

It is My Pleasure to Serve You
Roberta, Patient Coordinator

"I am thrilled to be part of a customer service team. Prior to dentistry, I worked as a customer service representative in the automotive industry for twenty-six years. What I love about working in dentistry is that I personally have the enjoyment of seeing the happiness that a fantastic customer service experience brings to a new patient's treatment experience.

"The first time I saw young patients getting their braces, their expression of excitement, joy, and happiness—I almost cried! It is very rewarding to be part of such a positive and special experience in a young person's life.

"As patient coordinator, my main job is to answer the phone and schedule appointments. I also take care of the patient's needs, asking 'How did we do today?' I also schedule all of the patient's future appointments and referrals. I am extremely reliable and a rock of trust that my team can always count on to get the job done. I coordinate appointments with the general dentist and other dental specialists, and I schedule wire removal for the patient's hygiene appointments. I am happy to serve the patient in any way that I can, and provide them with the highest quality orthodontic care and personalized customer service."

An Adoring Fan

When you solve a patient's problems, they become an enthusiastic, lifelong fan. Nowhere is this more evident than with rework of dental and orthodontic treatment. Sadly, these opportunities exist in dentistry. Whether it be redoing orthodontic treatment or cutting off thick ugly crowns made over crooked teeth, dentists and specialists are redoing dentistry that could have been done correctly the first time.

Dentists who help these unfortunate patients are customer service heroes. The financial reward for helping these patients is often far less than that earned by the dentist who did the poor dental work in the first place. Redo dentists help their patients for another reason; they truly care for their patients. These dentists put the patient first, before themselves. These are the dentists whose sole focus is "the thriving patient."

Let's all be dental heroes. Let's do dentistry right the first time and give our patients the highest quality of dental care that exists. Let's all earn the reward of patient fulfillment.

Chapter 18
CREATIVITY

Creativity is the power to connect the seemingly unconnected.
-William Plomer

One common theme of outstanding dental offices is that they are creative. When you enter, you usually hear conversation and laughter. They are having fun and you are invited to the party. Whether it's playing guitar, singing a song, wearing hats, holding up a smiley face, or putting on a red nose, memorable and remarkable customer service dental offices have doctor leadership and team members who are fully engaged in the customer service culture, care, and climate.

Happy customers will be emotionally moved by personal and creative entertainment. The best example I have seen of creativity of customer service in action is the orthodontic office of Dr. Jay Bowman, from Kalamazoo Orthodontics. *Star Wars'* Yoda tells children to wear their retainers. Community sports memorabilia lines the walls. Patients smile ear to ear with delight at the opportunity to take part in this unique office environment of fun. Dr. Bowman is a customer service creativity rock star.

As I write this book, I see Dr. Bowman and his patients on Facebook celebrating the Kalamazoo Orthodontics Patient Appreciation Movie Morning during Christmas break 2016. Dr. Bowman and a few hundred of his patients are at the new *Star Wars* movie, *Rogue One*. Dr. Bowman is dressed in an orange space jump-suit and his team members are dressed as an assortment of *Star Wars* characters, including Luke, Princess Leia,

CREATIVITY

Darth Vader, Yoda, and others. This event is nothing short of remarkable. I wish I could go to Dr. Bowman's office for orthodontic treatment!

I've never read a Yelp review that read, "I love your up-to-date computer software," or, "That new imaging system is fantastic!" I have read five-star Yelp reviews that say, "As a kid, what I remember most were the flavored gloves. I just loved those flavored gloves!"

Patients love the smallest things, the colorful items that make your office unique. These special gestures can be memorable, like the surprise of a birthday gift.

In my practice hometown of Antioch, California, the *Antioch Herald* printed the 2016 People's Choice Awards for orthodontists in our community. I am happy to report that we got a silver medal. Of course, I wanted gold. The woman who won gold, Dr. Shelby Smith, truly deserves recognition. She is remarkable. She offers a unique experience by bringing to her practice her cute little therapy dog, an adorable dachshund named PollyAnna.

Everyone adores puppies! The world's cutest dog, the renowned puppy by the name of Boo, has 17 million friends on Facebook. No human can compete with this level of popularity. Who else could deliver such an adorable and fluffy face?

I joined the puppy people and got some stuffed puppies for my office. This is the least that I could do. I give these "pets" away to the kids at the initial orthodontic evaluation. If you want to put smiles on youngsters' faces, spread some puppy love. Maybe next year I'll get People's Choice gold!

GIFTS OF APPRECIATION

Small gifts of appreciation make your customers feel special. For an instant, the recipient feels like a VIP. I will never forget reading about a remarkable customer experience written by Likeable's marketing guru Dave Kerpen in his book, *Likeable Leadership*. Kerpen describes a salad café in New York City with a long line. If you are a regular customer, you get your very own special little plastic bowl. If you returned with this special bowl, you move to the front of the line. Instantly, you become a VIP! Suddenly, everyone wants that plastic bowl! It is a mark of distinction, as well as a sign of owner appreciation. With that plastic bowl you can go places! These bowl-people are special. They're members of an Insider's Club.

Curious, I visited this unique salad café in New York City. It's true. I received a special orange salad bowl in which my custom salad was placed. Everyone received the special plastic bowl. It was their choice whether or not they chose to bring it back. I will always treasure this bowl as a fond memento of the experience.

Further down the avenues in New York City, I found the infamous soup man of the hit TV show *Seinfeld*. In these episodes, the aggressive and non-gracious soup man was known to say, "No soup for you!" Do we say this to our customers in our dental practices every time patients ask for something they want and we say, "No?" Or, do we exclude customers? When we create outsiders, we lose. This is a customer service failure.

How could you create engagement activities to include all of your customers past, present, and future, igniting your customer service experience? The orange plastic bowl possibilities are endless. Creativity leads to customer surprise, delight, and economic growth. Test as many ideas as you dare to find your true gems. Devote some time at your team meetings for creative customer service brainstorming. Develop patient VIP experiences and create loyal practice insiders.

OFFICE CHEERLEADERS

> *Customers will never love a company*
> *until the employees love it first.*
> -Simon Sinek

Done is better than perfect. Whatever wonderful new initiatives you and your creative team undertake, results will not always be perfect. It is the first time you have ever done it! You will need a positive attitude to get things rolling. The most important thing is to get started. You need office cheerleaders!

Creativity requires a positive attitude to overcome the inertia of implementation. I will never forget my first trial of decorating our office for "Smile Day." I had learned from orthodontist Dr. Donna Panucci of West Virginia changing office décor approximately every eight weeks was a great way to keep patients engaged. Although we had discussed this effort at our team meetings, we were having trouble getting someone to take charge. Finally, as the leader, I decided to take over, lead the way, and do it myself.

When the office was closed on a Monday, I prepared "Smile Day." I decorated in yellow with bright yellow floral arrangements, smiley faces, cheerleader pompoms, and balloons. Yellow take-away items were purchased, including pens, pencils, and wristbands. The children's treasure chest was refreshed with yellow bouncy balls, plushies, and toys. The team members all got new yellow shirts that day. We ordered smiley face stickers for every patient to receive. I printed the poem "Take Home a Smile" on yellow paper to give to each patient and parent as a souvenir of their special visit to our remarkable office.

Surprise! The team entered. Everyone was amazed at what we had created. We gathered as a group for the morning huddle. We put smiley face stickers on our clinic jackets and stocked up with stickers to give each patient that day. We all did it with excitement and enthusiasm. All except for one of us.

Then it came like a dark cloud over the Macy's Thanksgiving Day Parade—the words uttered with the energy of Eeyore, the slow donkey in the popular children's cartoon *Winnie the Pooh:* "I don't want to do it…"

"What?!" I said.

"I don't want to put the smiley face sticker on my jacket," came the negative response of one kill-joy team member.

"Then you're fired," was the response that came out of my mouth. I wish I hadn't said it, yet it was effective. The sticker quickly went on the team member's jacket but it was clear to all of us that this team member had a negative attitude, and a lack of enthusiasm. This employee was not interested in making the office the best that it could be. She was not a team player, and she did not choose to focus on our patients. She was a customer service killer!

This team member lasted another two weeks before she quit. She accepted a job at another dental office. She lasted there about two days. Then she left dentistry altogether.

You need office cheerleaders to make your customer service work. Your team is the backbone of your customer service delivery system. All team members are central to the vision and the plan. Occasionally you may need to weed-out those who seek to choke customer service. Don't let anyone rain on your customer service parade!

Creating Happiness

Always give the customer more than they expect.
-Nelson Boswell

Happiness is the product and reward of great customer service. Don't be afraid to invite patients to your party. Start the small-talk conversation, ask a patient to pose for a VIP photo on Facebook, or invite all to join in on the latest contest. Engaged patients become part of your dental office family.

Making another person happy returns happiness to the giver, creating a joyful environment. This is the Sunshine Boomerang Effect. Make this phenomenon part of your everyday practice culture.

You may want to express your creativity through custom patient programs. These could include an Invisalign Day, an Adult Patient Day, a Massage Day, a New Patient Day, or a Braces Off Day. Whatever your bright idea, doing something special will bring the team together and make your office patient-centric. Put on your thinking caps! What can you come up with? Start one initiative today. Five-star customer service is all about surprise and delight.

Innovation

Innovators are creators of surprise and delight. Comprising just 2.5 percent of the population, these are the people who are not afraid to try something new and daring. They're the people who bring fresh perspectives and ideas to your dental practice.

You are probably one of those brilliant and charismatic people. If you are the leader, you may also have such a person on your team. Take care to identify, foster, and promote the innovators in your midst!

Try this exercise with your team. Ask everyone to list twelve items about your dental practice that denote outstanding care, a service culture, a positive and fun climate, making you unique, and your patients feeling special. Here is a sample list:

1. New patient welcome signs
2. New patient whoopie pies
3. Chocolate chip cookies

CREATIVITY

4. Whitening trays for engaged couples and beauty contestants
5. Warm face towels
6. Sugarless gum at the front desk
7. Annual Patient Appreciation Party
8. Fresh fruit with a chocolate fountain
9. Patient art calendar
10. Gifts for school classrooms
11. Girl Scouts and Boy Scouts office field trip
12. Doctor speaker events: school, Rotary, Chamber of Commerce, City Council, PTA

The possibilities are limitless. Use your brain power to innovate your way to success with some original events that are fun for patients, their family and friends, and the team.

Ephemera

*It is the service we are not obliged to give
that people value most.*
-J. C. Penney

"What's up with all the ephemera (simply put, the "stuff") in dentistry? Who doesn't love getting a little gift? Marketers know that "free" is the most powerful word in product promotion. Dental offices should be filled with logo items that turn your patients into instant word-of-mouth marketers for your practice. Why do we do it? Because it works!

Have you ever received a dessert compliments of the chef? If this small piece of tasty joy does not produce instant happiness, I don't know what will! Surprise and delight! It can be the same in your dental office. I once gave out bananas in March for National Nutrition Month. Patients were smiling from ear to ear. Make each day unique. If you do, your patients will look forward to coming back, time and time again.

What would make teachers come out of their classrooms to make a request for themselves and their family when a dentist visits their local school? The light-up toothbrush! This small superstar item puts an instant smile on the face of every child, every teacher, and every parent. I still have never experienced any excitement quite like it!

At Gorczyca Orthodontics, we give each new patient the Crest Oral B OrthoEssentials oral hygiene kit as a new patient start gift. By receiving a beautiful package like it is Christmas or their birthday, the patient feels appreciated and special. We are giving our patients the gift of oral health. This is, after all, the goal of every dentist: to have every patient in great oral health, with excellent oral hygiene, free of cavities and gingivitis.

Office T-shirts make your patients part of your office family and your internal marketing team. Patients in your practice T-shirts become walking bulletin boards for your dental practice in the community. Is your office T-shirt worthy? Try it and see. Your patients will love wearing your office T-shirt and recommending you to others.

My sister, an internal medicine physician, gives a children's book to each child to read and keep when they accompany their parent to their medical appointment in her office. When one of these children returned years later, now as her adult patient, he recalled to her how much receiving that book had meant to him as a child. He still treasured this special gesture from decades earlier and specifically chose her as his medical doctor.

Office Themes

At Gorczyca Orthodontics, we aim to remain contemporary with the times by constantly highlighting popular culture. This is especially important with kids. Take time to ask the kids themselves (or your own children) what kids like. My eleven-year-old son is my "Director of Marketing." Contemporary items and decor help dentists and team members bridge the gap with the youngest generation and make your office a fun, kid-friendly place.

Your up-to-date themes may reflect holidays, movies, or popular personalities. Special campaigns may be run such as, "Mom's My Hero," or "Dad's My Hero," so as to include parents. Add pictures of your patients hugging Mom or Dad, or have a "Lovefest" contest. Unique promotions cause the excitement to build!

If you need office theme ideas, they may be purchased in a box from the marketing and social media company, My Social Practice. Find them at www.mysocialpractice.com. You will never be without ideas for posts, contests, and fun-filled events.

DECORATIONS

At Gorczyca Orthodontics, we decorate our office with a Hawaiian beach theme in the summer to complement our "Summer Splash" Patient Appreciation Party theme. Palm trees and floral leis are everywhere. Grass skirts line the clinic walls. Smiley face beach balls lie atop our shelves. We dress in tropical colors of pink, yellow, orange, and lime green. If someone cannot personally go to Hawaii, one of the happiest states, they can at least dream about the experience in our orthodontic office during their appointment. One cannot help but walk into our office and think, *Aloha! They're having fun around here!*

Little boys love Minecraft. I am well aware of this fact because of my young son. The Minecraft character Steve and his creatures have various entertaining activities that delight and fascinate children for hours. If only dentistry could be so entertaining! We can at least decorate certain rooms with a Minecraft poster to help entertain these young minds.

Try having a kid-friendly office theme that changes every two to three years. Spanning back twenty years, our themes have included Minecraft, One Direction, Justin Bieber, Disney, Hannah Montana, High School Musical, Harry Potter, Backstreet Boys, Pokémon, Beanie Babies, and even the Spice Girls! My personal favorite theme has always been the yellow smiley face. Perhaps yellow is the theme of this book as the smiley face is the happiness product of customer service. I love the color yellow, smiley faces, and making people smile. You will, too!

Chapter 19

PRESERVATION

Caring is your number one competitive edge.
-Tom Peters

The most difficult part of customer service excellence is this: preservation of systems. Known as "Management of Systems," you must, on a consistent basis, preserve the details of your customer service experience. Five-star customer service excellence takes hard work to achieve, but it takes constant, and daily attention to maintain.

Customer service leaders will come and go. Team members change. You will need to continue to train and retrain, collect feedback, and address necessary improvements. Every day there will be a new challenge. You will need to consistently revisit, as a team, your vision, goals, and mission.

PERSEVERANCE

*We must earn the right
to our continued relationship with customers.*
-Jeanne Bliss

Don't kid yourself. Dealing with customers can be tough, especially in the dental office. Patients may already be tense about their dental procedure. They may have fear. They may be stressed about the high cost of dentistry. They may also have personal and emotional problems. And there you are, the front-line customer service leader, dealing with all of these issues. It's not easy.

Every once in a while, patients are going to direct their pent-up anger and frustration at you. When this happens, take a deep breath and stay calm. Keep a smile on your face and remind yourself that you are there to serve the patient. Be pleasant and persevere.

When you become the direct beneficiary of your customer's frustration, pick yourself up, dust yourself off, and let it go. Squeeze your smiley face stress ball. Think a happy thought and be thankful that you have a job. Remind yourself of how you are able to help this patient. Here are some tips that may help you during a difficult time or situation.

Four Tips for Handling Customer Stress

Make the customer's problem your problem.
-Shep Hyken

1. REMEMBER YOUR CORE VALUES, MISSION, MANTRAS, AND VISION

   These affirmative statements will remind you of your purpose and inspire you with the "why" of doing what you do.

2. SET A SMALL GOAL OF CONTINUED SERVICE

   Anything that you can do to help or please the customer should be done. It could be making a call, sending a card, giving a gift, or sending flowers. If nothing else, it will give you the satisfaction of knowing that you have done everything possible to let the patient know that you care.

3. TRY SOMETHING NEW

   If all efforts fail, tell the patient that you want them to be happy. Perhaps they would be happier somewhere else. But this option is always the very last resort.

   I will never forget a very unhappy mother of a patient that I once had in my orthodontic office. No matter what I did, she would complain. Finally, I said, "I want you to be happy. It is very obvious that no matter what I do, you are unhappy in our office. You deserve to be happy. So here's what we're going to do. We are going to gather your daughter's orthodontic records and have them ready for you at 5:00 p.m. today. Please come pick them up and let us know which of the other orthodontic offices in town will be finishing your daughter's orthodontic treatment."

At 5:00 p.m. a telephone call came. Mom stated, "I'm really sorry, Dr. Gorczyca. I really am happy in your office and I don't want to go anywhere else. It's just that I'm a single mom and it's hard for me to deal with my teenage daughter, take time off of work to get to the appointments, and arrive in time before closing because of rush-hour traffic. It's not you, it's me."

This may also be the case for you in your dental office.

4. TRY, TRY, and TRY AGAIN

Learn from your mistakes and never stop trying. Mirror best practices techniques. Read books, listen to consultants, and hang out in customer service chat rooms. Try new things. Undertake novel strategies. Make it part of your office climate.

Remember Who's the Boss

There is only one boss: the customer.
And he can fire everybody in the company
from the chairman on down,
simply by spending his money somewhere else.
-Sam Walton

Who's the boss? The customer. In dentistry, it is the patient and their family. You will need to continue to treat your patients as if it were the first time you ever served them. You can never let up on attention to the customer. You must truly listen to your patients to receive continual feedback. Always remember that the customer makes your job possible.

MEASUREMENTS

What gets measured gets improved.
-Peter Drucker

Goals achieved can be recorded by measurements. Feedback, comments, and surveys will need consistent review. To measure customer service, consider collecting and assessing data.

FOUR CUSTOMER SERVICE MEASUREMENTS

1. PHONE CALLS ANSWERED

    Do you know what percentage of your phone calls are answered on the first or second ring? Do you know what percentage of phone calls go to voice mail? This can be monitored by a voice tracking system. This technology is available via marketing companies such as Affordable Image, a professional marketing company, or from the Valpak mailer.

    Recorded phone calls can also be reviewed for politeness, efficiency, success in documentation of the customer name and phone number, and conversion rate into new patient exams and treatment starts.

    For tracking phone data in your dental office, use a new call-in number for each promotional campaign. Count the number and outcome of calls to assess your mailing effectiveness. The facts vital to your practice become readily apparent. The first is the day and time when most new patient calls are most frequently made. Our results revealed that 8:00 a.m. to 9:00 a.m. and 12:00 p.m. to 1:00 p.m. are the most popular times. This reveals the most popular day for new patient calls. Our data has revealed Tuesdays.

2. SAME DAY STARTS

    New patients take time from work and school to schedule exam appointments. How many of these appointments accomplish something the same day as the initial exam? Offering same day treatment is a great service to the patient, saving them time and money. This option is also an incredible practice builder. Staying late to start a new case means going the extra mile, delighting the patient and their family. Coming in early or working through lunch is just as valuable. Give 100 percent effort to building your practice by accommodating exams and treatment starts the same day that the patient calls.

3. "WILL CALL" STARTS

   What percentage of exams or non-same-day starts return to start treatment in your office? Do you follow-up effectively in calling these patients? What percentage of your patients who say that they "will call" actually do so? Do you stay in contact?

   I am amazed at the number of patients who years after their initial exam return for orthodontic treatment. Orthodontist Donna Galante, in her book *The Millimeter Approach* suggests staying in touch with new patients for six years before determining that they will not follow through with treatment. Consistent communication will only increase your conversion rate and the likelihood of the new patient starting treatment in your office.

4. YOUR CUSTOMER SERVICE RATING

   In your office customer service surveys, what percentage of your patients are giving you five-star reviews both in the office and on the Internet? Tally up your scores. Are you five-star ninety percent of the time or something less? Work to improve this score and address areas that could be improved.

Safety

> *At the end of the day, the goals are simple:*
> *safety and security.*
> -Jodi Rell

Psychologist Abraham Maslow ranked safety and security as the second most important human need after physiological satisfaction. Personal security and avoidance of personal harm is important for yourself, your loved ones, your friends, and especially for your patients.

In the preservation of customer service, safety ranks first. You must always provide for the welfare, comfort, and peace of mind of each patient. Each team member is responsible for their own safety as well as for the well-being of others. The goal is a safe, secure, and accident-free environment and office.

Dental equipment must constantly be maintained and used properly. Teammates are responsible for themselves, their patients, and their co-workers. Everyone deserves to work with skilled, careful technicians in an accident-averse setting.

Safety is a service standard; it is also the subject of local, state, and federal regulations. Safety takes patience, care, and attention to detail. It is each team member's responsibility to maintain their health and safety. A patient cannot get poked, knocked, stabbed, elbowed, or have chemical or dental debris accidently sprayed into their throat or eyes. Anesthesia adds additional liability. Everything in the vicinity of the patient matters. A safe workplace is the reflection of good choices.

Patient Eyes

Protect your patients from the unfortunate incident of something dropping into their eye during a dental procedure. Protective goggles, glasses, or sunglasses worn by the patient during procedures ensure dental patient eye safety. During preps with a high-speed hand piece, debris can fly through the air at 50 to 60 mph. Have your dental patient wear protective eyewear when cutting old restorations. Have your assistant holding the high-speed suction for patient comfort and protection.

You may want to give your patient a pair of groovy sunglasses with your office logo. The patient can take the sunglasses home with them after the procedure. During long procedures, you can offer virtual reality goggles with video games or movies downloaded from Netflix.

Take care to make chairside retainer or temporary crown adjustments below the level of the patient's eyes. Your patient may be laying back in the dental chair. Prevent debris from flying in the direction of your patient's face by keeping your hands low and by turning to the side, away from your patient.

Escorting Patients

Politely escort patients and do not point. This is a common but necessary courtesy in such a confined area as a dental office. You may want to escort elderly patients out of the building and to their car after a long dental procedure. This non-random act of kindness may prevent them from slipping or falling. Place patients in a wheelchair when necessary, especially after oral surgical procedures when the patient was sedated.

Floors and Sidewalks

Floors are the number one indoor hazard related to customer safety. Liquid spills, rain water brought in on umbrellas or shoes, or water spray hitting the floor in a dental lab or bathroom are accident traps waiting to happen. Pay attention, and wipe up spills immediately.

Carpeting is still the most desirable floor covering for patient safety in the dental office. Carpeting also creates a quiet environment. Watch for trip hazards like toys or games dropped by children. Make sure that the floors are clear of objects that could cause tripping and falling. Do not allow bare feet in your office.

Moisture of any kind on hard floors, from mopping or other sources, is problematic. Wet floors are a major liability, which could lead to a worker's compensation claim or personal injury. Mop floors after hours and use professional cleaning services when possible.

Sidewalks also can be a source of liability. Sweeping the sidewalks regularly will ensure that there are no hazards on which patients and their families could trip. Sidewalks must be cleared of fallen branches, leaves, sand, stones, or lose masonry and litter on which patients might trip.

Overall maintenance reflects your brand. Be sure that all walking surfaces both inside and outside the office are safe. Eliminate cracks and breaks in the sidewalks, tiles, or carpeting. Keep your office and grounds as good as brand new.

Health Safety

*Out of clutter
find simplicity.*
-Albert Einstein

An uncluttered office will reassure the patient that attention to detail is being made in all areas of dental healthcare including protection against cross-contamination. Keep countertops clean and spray and polish surfaces frequently throughout the day. Appoint an office cleanliness coordinator.

Patients will be evaluating everything you do, everything you touch, and everything they see to ensure a clean and healthy office. Cleanliness helps maximize the patient's positive perception of your office brand and dental care experience. Patients know clean and healthy when they see it. Devote time and attention to keeping your office clean, changing your gloves often, and keeping your environment healthy for both your patients and those who work in your dental office.

Cross-Contamination

In the dental office, it is important to remember to place barriers and to prevent cross-contamination. Patients will be watching the doctors' and assistants' use of gloves. Gloves must be removed and left on the patient tray when leaving the chair. Instruments need to be clean and opened in front of the patient. Autoclave validations need to be documented. OSHA continuing education must be completed on the regular or monthly basis. Hand-washing and use of alcohol-based cleanser in between patients is critical. Surface disinfectant cleaner, disinfectant, deodorizer, tuberculocidal, virucidal, bactericidal, fungicidal products are the basis of all day continuing education and will not be discussed in detail here. It is, however, important to realize that this critical subject is a vital part of customer service.

Medical Safety

As you review your dental patient's medical history, you may find that your patient may be without a physician or in need of a physician. Refer immediately if you feel your dental patient is having health issues beyond the scope of dentistry.

Review your patient's medical history thoroughly and update it every two years. If you find an elevated blood pressure when administering anesthetic, refer the patient to a physician immediately. Avoid having elderly patients get up too quickly from the dental chair. For patients with neck or back conditions, take care to provide pillows for comfortable position, especially for long procedures.

Children's Play Area

If your office has a children's play area in the reception area, be sure that toys are not left spread about on the floor. Be sure to remove all sharp edges on walls, cabinets, and doors.

I once worked in a large group practice that had such a play area. Its doors were a very beautiful polished metal but this surface had sharp edges. One day, a little girl slipped and hit her head on the edge of the door frame: the resultant forehead laceration required sutures. Consider rubber edge liners in children's play areas and children's safety in the selection of the materials you add to your dental office.

Environment

Guard your office environment. This would include prohibiting unwanted visits by people who should not have open access to your office. This might include random visits of team member boyfriends, friends, or family members who have no business in the office. It could be the husband or ex-husband of one of your assistants. Personal visitors should not be allowed in the office during normal service hours or even after hours when they can detract from patient care or office management. These distractions could become an additional office liability.

Personal phone calls need to be kept to a minimum during work hours. One personal phone call per day to allow a working mother to know what her children are doing after school is acceptable. You do not want unnecessary personal calls tying up the phone lines and taking attention away from patient calls. Private cell phones should be put away and out of reach when attending to patients. Emergency phone calls to team members should be made to the office backline whenever possible.

Property

Protect all office property. This includes intellectual property such as training materials, handouts, manuals, schedules, and procedures. Private property should also be properly stored.

Equipment property will need maintenance, which is not a topic to be discussed openly, in front of patients. Such discussion may reduce patient ease. Instrument function, maintenance, and repair are best to be completed on non-patient days, whenever possible.

Those who use your expensive and sensitive dental computer systems will need to be well- trained. Everyone with computer access must have an individual entry User Name and hardened Password. Don't allow your business computer to be used for personal use. The risk of infection by viruses is high. Even worse, your system could be hacked. Restrict your office computer solely for office function.

Your Office Lease

> *Great service is never static,*
> *it's always dynamic.*
> -Jim Williamson

Protection of the physical aspects of your building, whether you own or rent, is everyone's responsibility. Your building, your office, and your physical space will need constant maintenance, both inside and out. Grounds need to be swept. The parking lot needs to be well-lit. Plants will need to be watered and trees trimmed. These are the activities of routine building maintenance.

Do you know a dentist who has lost their lease, and in haste is forced to scramble for a new office space? Or, a dentist who never renegotiates their lease and their monthly rent is through the roof? If you are a dentist, you will need to start early to renew your lease. Renegotiation is best started two years before lease expiration. This ensures that you have renegotiation power with the landlord and time to move out of the building if need be.

The cost of professional building rent has actually gone down in the last fourteen years. Take this economic trend opportunity to start renegotiating your lease for better and lower terms. Hire a professional.

Personally, I have been successful renegotiating my lease with the services of George Vaill, www.georgevaill.com, a professional dental office lease re-negotiator. We started renegotiating terms of my lease two years prior to the due date. Mr. Vaill and his team were able to reduce my rent and common area maintenance fee by thirty-three percent, delivering a personal savings of $125,000 over the next seven years.

You have no guarantee that your landlord will renew your lease. You will need a long lease and renewal contract in the sale of your office. This is of utmost importance to the buyer and the bank, which will offer the loan to the purchaser of your practice. Be prepared for every scenario and set yourself up for success by the preservation of your dental office space lease.

Reputation

> *Get the right people on the bus*
> *and the wrong people off the bus.*
> -Jim Collins

The reputation of your dental office is ensured when all team members are "all in." These team members must be devoted to the office and happy to be working there. Protecting the excellent customer service brand of your office must also be everyone's goal. If someone speaks poorly of your dental office under their breath, or more openly, this is organizational betrayal. Address such behavior immediately and eliminate it. If someone says, "I think I'll quit," take it at face-value that they are uncommitted to your customer service goals, your patients, and your office.

Team members must always speak positively about the dental office in which you work. Truthful and open communication of concerns will lead to improvement. Have a team rule that, "Only the truth shall be spoken." If there is a customer service breech, everyone needs to know about it right away.

Insubordination toward serving the customer is grounds for immediate termination. Be clear that everyone is there to improve the office, making it the best that it can be. If someone feels that they don't belong on the team, or they are not dedicated to your customer service or your office mission, vision, and goals, they need to go. Nothing is as difficult and emotionally charged as shepherding your customer service team through the process of human resource management. It is, however, one of the backbone elements of the preservation of your customer service climate, care, and culture.

Fight for the protection of the professional reputation of your office. When the reputation of the office is threatened, everyone who is employed by your office needs to do whatever he or she can do to rectify the situation. The activities within the practice should, at all times, remain professional. Reflect the quality of customer service care that is the office standard.

Violation of appropriate professional conduct would include proprietary activities or services in the office. This would include activities that have nothing to do with patient care. An example would be a cosmetics sale or even Girl Scout cookies. Although fun, this type of distraction will reduce the office reputation to that of a flea market.

A Fun Work and Patient Climate

There are not employees here,
only internal customers.
-Einstein Medical Center

Google allocates twenty percent of worker time for creative projects. Look for, create, and discover ways to make your office more enjoyable. If you do, everyone will want to work at your dental office, dentists and patients will keep sending you referrals, and all of your patients will love visiting you. Patients and families will look forward to their dental appointments.

There are so many things you can do in your dental office that are just plain fun! Be creative. Some activities could include telling jokes, giving Valentine's Day cards, exchanging friendship bracelets, serving cupcakes, giving bananas, handing out T-shirts and caps, taking pictures, giving a small gift, and sponsoring contests, parties, or open houses. Surprises make your customer feel appreciated. Freebies, gift cards, giveaways, or personalized thank you notes will make your office unique and memorable. A thank you rose or a $5 Starbucks gift card are sure to delight a busy mom. All of these things make your patients feel special. They build patient relationships and make your workplace enjoyable.

It is essential that your employees enjoy work, feel appreciated, and are happy to be able to delight patients. Your goal is to have team members who are at ease, comfortable, and able to enjoy each other's company. Team cohesion will fuel magical patient experiences and make your dental office a place of joy and service to your patients.

When you smile, your team smiles, and your customers smile as well. So lighten up! Tell some stories. Tell some jokes. Decorate the office. Surprise and delight your customers. Have fun!

Chapter 20

FIVE-STAR CUSTOMER SERVICE

*The goal as a company is
to have customer service that is not just the best
but legendary.*
-Sam Walton

Two thousand years ago in the conquered Roman territories of Judea in what is now known as Israel, Jewish boys were required by Roman law to carry the soldiers' backpacks for one mile. This was an extraordinary feat, considering that these backpacks weighed sixty to seventy pounds. If the Jewish boy refused, it could be grounds for his immediate death.

In an act of courage, character, and pride of a dominated people, the Rabbis of the land sent out an edict. When you are done with your long, hard mile, politely ask, "Could I carry this an extra mile for you?" The Jewish boy was now in control. This boy could choose, of his own free will, to go the extra mile.

"Going the extra mile" means great service. Giving customer service all you've got, and delivering outstanding care to individual wants and needs, is going the extra mile. The origins of these words mean all that and a lot more.

Going the Extra Mile

*The key is to set realistic customer expectations,
and then not to just meet them, but to exceed them—
preferably in unexpected and helpful ways.*
-Richard Branson

Are we willing to go the extra mile for our patients? There is not much competition when you personally choose to do unexpected things for your patients in the present moment, making a personal sacrifice of time and attention in service to others.

You need not own the dental practice, or be a millionaire, PhD, president, or manager of a Fortune 500 company to go the extra mile. You just need to be humble, unassuming, hardworking, and to care about other people more than yourself when serving others. You need to want to be more than average in the care and service you provide.

Going the extra mile can apply to everything that you do in life as well as in the dental office. Going the extra mile could apply to helping a co-worker when they feel stressed or overwhelmed. It could apply to cleaning the office without being asked. It could mean staying late to treat one last emergency patient or accommodating one additional patient procedure that evening.

Each time you come in contact with a dental patient, you have the opportunity to deliver five- star customer service. This is a frame of mind. It is about serving the individual, not the masses. It is not about being all things to all people: it's about doing specific things for specific people.

By asking, listening, and personally knowing individual likes and dislikes, you make each patient feel special, heard, and individually cared for. Take note of what your patients love so you can delight them with their own interests. Start at the initial exam. Have a patient preference "Getting to Know You" questionnaire asking each patient about their passions, family, and pastimes. Shared interests and common understanding make the difference in building a relationship. Knowing your patient personally is priceless.

Small Acts of Kindness

> *We wildly underestimate the power
> of the tiniest personal touch.*
> -Tom Peters

Customer service coach Tal Shnall recalls first learning hospitality from his mother in Israel. A master hostess in her own home, she taught him three important lessons of customer service, which he still uses today in his own hospitality coaching at top hotel brands including Marriott, Hilton, Starwood, and Intercontinental Hotels. These three essentials serve as a review for five-star customer service.

Three Customer Service Essentials

> *Before you go the extra mile for your customers,
> ask in which direction they would like to go.*
> -Nicholas C. Hill

1. GREET PEOPLE WITH A SMILE

Never underestimate the power of your smile when greeting patients. People want to feel positive and energized by the people with whom they do business. Your own happiness, appearance, and smile sets the tone for your business interaction with your customers.

2. ADD VALUE TO THE EXPERIENCE

Beyond the customer visit, offering coffee, tea, or other beverages will make your patient feel at home. You want your customers to feel like special friends and guests, and to know that they are valued by you and your team as people. Take time to ask your customers what they would like and how best to serve them. Surprising and delighting your guests by offering something extra will help your guests enjoy their experience at your business.

3. MAKE A GOOD FIRST IMPRESSION FOR A GOOD LAST IMPRESSION

A good first impression is the beginning of a successful relationship. This is where organization, planning, and forethought pay off. Essential to this is that your dental office be immaculately clean. Next, you want your warm welcome to occur as planned. Let your new customer know that they are the most important person in the room. When your guests feel appreciated, they will keep coming back. You want your customers to know how much you truly care.

These are the golden principles of hospitality. Little things go a long way. We all need recognition in our daily lives. This is what every human being craves. Interaction is a validation that we matter. Every kindness and small acknowledgement makes a difference in the lives of others. Customer service is not about you. It is about the inspiration and service that you give to others.

Greeting a patient by name asking, "How are things today?" and taking time to have a personal conversation are the essence of the customer experience. Keep asking questions. Physical acts of looking your patients in the eye, smiling, shaking hands, saying thank you, or giving a fond farewell add a personal touch. Make your dental office visit a bright moment in your patient's day.

In Walnut Creek, California, there is a family-owned jewelry store, Davidson & Licht, which offers guest concierge service. A man in a uniform including white gloves personally greets customers at the door. After opening the door, he next offers customers water served in a custom labeled bottle along with a candied orange slice served on a silver platter. His presence is like a "Welcome home" to returning customers. Tiffany's is right down the street but its level of service cannot compare to this one-of-a-kind establishment. It can be the same for you in your dental practice. We can easily do this for our dental patients.

When we consistently give our patients a new toothbrush, toothpaste, and floss in their "Goody Bag" or a pack of sugarless gum or ChapStick, it is their special treat. These tokens of care make the visit memorable. Your patients will continue to look forward to these small acts of kindness at their next dental appointment.

Legendary Customer Service

*There is a big difference between a
satisfied customer and a loyal customer.*
-Shep Hyken

My husband and I often travel great distances to medical and dental conferences. My most memorable customer service experience occurred in Hamburg, Germany, at the Hotel Altar. After many hours of travel, my husband and I were weary, but we were anticipating a fantastic conference and mini vacation. At the Hotel Vier Jahreseiten, in Hamburg, we were pleasantly surprised to be personally escorted to our room. We were entranced by the view of the Alster River and its canals outside of our hotel window.

Suddenly, the doorbell rang. It was room service with a bottle of champagne, fruit, and chocolate. My husband and I looked at each other in amazement and asked, "Did you order this?" The gentleman stated, "Compliments of the house, Madam."

I asked, "How did you know?"

The man simply responded with a smile, bowing politely. All we could say was, "Wow!" Talk about an outstanding first impression! I still remember this occasion with joy to this day, nearly fifteen years later.

Outstanding five-star customer service is memorable. It is legendary. If you deliver five-star customer service, it inspires your patients to talk about you in the community and refer others to you for years to come. Being remarkable and unforgettable is the art of customer service.

The Platinum Rule

*It's easier to love a brand
when the brand loves you back.*
-Seth Godin

We all know the golden rule: treat others as you would like to be treated. For legendary five-star customer service, take it a step further. Go for the platinum rule: treat others as *they* wish to be treated. Doing so will require anticipation of their needs and fulfillment of even their unexpressed desires.

Staying True to Five-Star Values

*Revolve your world around the customer
and more customers will revolve around you.*
-Heather Williams

At a five-star level of treatment, patients go beyond feeling very satisfied and having their expectations exceeded; they are truly delighted. A fundamental key to five-star service is an ability to read the guest accurately, to give them what they desire.

I once completed orthodontic examinations on a family of five: mother, father, and three daughters. After reviewing the diagnosis and treatment plans with the family, Dad asked, "If we choose this office, will we win an iPad?"

Surprised by this question, I responded, "We would be honored to have you here as patients at Gorczyca Orthodontics. You have our commitment to providing you with clinical excellence, outstanding customer service, and a great patient experience. We guarantee your satisfaction. We will take great care of you."

I then added, "No. You will not be receiving an iPad."

Dad replied, "Good. Then, we'll all get started."

Five-star servers understand the customer on a personal level. They make the patient feel heard and important, and they understand what the customer is truly asking for. Insincere fads and gimmicks will lessen the customer service experience, especially when pushed at the initial examination appointment. Imagine checking in to first class on a premiere airline and the first thing you're asked or given is information on how to enter a contest for a free trip to Aruba, or how to refer a family member or friend.

Five-star customer service is a philosophy that touches the human spirit. It makes patients feel important, heard, cared for, and hopefully, loved. When you back up your sincere care with concrete actions, patients can't help but fall in love with you. Putting your patients first will show them that you love your business of dentistry. Providing the best of everything—the best of clinical dentistry, the best services, and the best referrals for specialty care—will show your patients that you are in the profession to serve others, not just to make a living. By putting patients first, you differentiate your dental practice as one of excellence in serving others.

Five-Star Reviews

Five-star reviews are a treasure to your practice. Share your five-star reviews with your team, and let them inspire you. Make them part of your office culture. Read them at team meetings and post them on Facebook. You've earned them! Whatever your five-star reviews say, do more of that.

You are the customer service leader for your dental office. Your dental office success depends on you: what you do, what you say, and how you do it. You have been chosen by your patients, and Job #1 is to deliver a great and exceptional customer experience.

I hope this book has helped you understand and focus on customer service. The excitement in the opportunity to serve others will help you grow your personal fulfillment in the service to the profession of dentistry.

Customer Service is the New Marketing

If you build a great experience,
customers tell each other about that.
Word of mouth is very powerful.
-Jeff Bezos

Giving your customers personal attention is internal marketing at its finest. Customer service is a powerful marketing asset. It usually costs very little other than time and attention.

The return on investment of five-star customer service is valuable. Reports by the American Customer Service Satisfaction Index (http://www.theacsi.org/) show that companies which lead in customer service outperform the Dow by 93%, the Fortune 500 by 20%, and the NASDAQ by 335%! That's impressive!

Let Service Inspire Your Life

Only a life lived in service to others
is a life worth living.
-Albert Einstein

In the #1 National Bestseller *Outliers*, Malcolm Gladwell shares the history of New York doctors and lawyers who were descendants of immigrants to the US at the turn of the last century. He states that these "doctors and lawyers did not become professionals in spite of their humble origins. They became professional *because* of their humble origins."

Perhaps this is the case with customer service leaders. Customer service expert Shep Hyken writes that he first learned customer service from his parents; hospitality speaker Tal Shnall attributes his early customer service influence to his mother. Similarly, I first learned customer service from a family member, my grandmother. These are the cherished memories of service in a loving environment which continue to inspire us.

Next time your patient enters your dental office, imagine a sign above the door which reads, "Welcome to the dental world of outstanding customer service. Here you leave your world behind." Your customer has entered your world, which you have created especially for them.

Now you can write your own story of customer service. You decide how the story starts and ends, and all the minor details along the way. Your story is about you, your office, your brand, and your five-star customer service. Add to your story how you will make the world a better place, how you will help others by serving them, and what a difference you make in people's lives by your life-changing dental treatment. This is your "Why" of customer service. This is your foundation of your customer service journey.

Be something bigger than yourself. True success comes when we commit ourselves to helping others. Smiles change lives. Dentistry gives us this marvelous experience. And, your *At Your Service* journey of customer service is your greatest opportunity.

CONCLUSION

Success is turning knowledge into positive action.
– Dorothy Leeds

As customer service leaders, some of you are saying, "Hey, we could do that." Make things happen. Make a commitment right now to start implementing small changes to improve your customer service experience. Your increased awareness of dental office customer service opportunities will help you to master future challenges.

Customer service requires a leader and that leader is you. After reading this book, I hope that you will be able to handle customer service situations with finesse. You now know you are not alone in your daily challenges. Lastly, I hope that this book will contribute to your professional contentment and happiness.

We can do no great things, only small things with great love.
– Mother Teresa

Customer service is a reception. The guests are greeted. People socialize. Compliments are exchanged. Food and drinks are served. Gifts are given. The atmosphere is lite and enjoyable. The guests are delighted. It's a fun experience. Guests are thanked and given a fond farewell. If the reception feels like home, people will want to come back. Everyone will look forward to next time.

Outstanding customer service takes planning. It doesn't happen on its own. Reaching your customer service goals will take continuous focus,

CONCLUSION

communication, organization, and review. Each day, your customer service will improve. Every moment, you're on. It's Showtime. It's time for you to delight your patients. This ongoing effort is your customer service culture, care, and climate.

When your customers matter, your work matters, and you matter. Remember, you're "*At Your Service...*" for your customers. I hope this book has transformed your customer service relationship and has inspired you to go the extra mile for customers. I hope this book has also refreshed your approach to serving your patients. Take time now to write your own book and fill out the Customer Service Calendar Template which follows in Appendix 1. Here's to your success. Now, go out and serve.

Appendix 1

CUSTOMER SERVICE CALENDAR TEMPLATE

	Culture	**Care**	**Climate**
Jan			
Feb			
Mar			
Apr			
May			
June			
July			
Aug			
Sept			
Oct			
Nov			
Dec			

Appendix 2

SAMPLE CUSTOMER SERVICE CALENDAR

	Culture	**Care**	**Climate**
Jan	Pt. Wall of Fame	Welcome Sign	MRBIV/T3s
Feb	Annual Advance	Questionnaire	Office Clean-up
Mar	Mission	Prize Box	Current Magazines
Apr	Core Values	Flavored Gloves	Custom Folders
May	Business Cards	Hygiene Kit	Fragrance
June	10 Phrases	Pens and Pencils	Blanket Restock
July	Thank You Notes	Tokens and Prizes	Diagnostic Wax-Up
Aug	Small Talk	Appreciation Party	Debond Letter
Sept	Team Handbook	Contests	Patient Special Day
Oct	Dress Code	Debond Gift	Update Posters
Nov	Surveys	Before + After Photos	Safety Glasses
Dec	CSX Awards	Cards	Patient Gifts

ACKNOWLEDGEMENTS

Great service travels in circles.
-William Noyse

Books are built over time. This resource has been a personal labor of love for the creation of dental resources. It is the result of numerous years in clinical practice, with the resultant experiences, conversations, classes, resources, and collaboration among my colleagues and friends who care about orthodontics, dentistry, customer service, and dental practice management. Thanks to all of you for sharing your thoughts and experiences with me.

I am thankful to the people who made this book possible. Thank you to the excellent customer service leaders at Gorczyca Orthodontics, without whom patient care and customer service activities would not exist: Jolene, Veronica, Dana, Pam, Roberta, Gwen, and Patti. Thank you for your hard work and dedication to our customer service climate, care, and culture.

Thank you to Marianne Way for the initial transcription of this manuscript, as well as those of my first two books. I am so grateful to know you as a patient, transcriptionist, and friend.

Thank you to my dear friend orthodontist Dr. Maureen Valley, of Valley Orthodontics, San Rafael, California, who was my classmate at both Harvard School of Dental Medicine and the Harvard School of Public Health. Your passion for dental practice management and organization of the Practice Management Course as former orthodontic clinic director at the Arthur A. Dugoni School of Dentistry, University of the Pacific gave

ACKNOWLEDGEMENTS

birth to first a lecture, then a presentation, then my books. I owe you a debt of gratitude for the opportunity and inspiration which you gave me.

Thank you to Flavio Martins, author of the book *Win the Customer*, for your insightful foreword to this book and support of this project. Your customer service blog and excellent book are a great resource for everyone interested in pursuing excellence in customer service.

Thank you to Dr. David Moffet, best-selling author of *The Big Yellow Book of Dental Customer Service*, for his friendship, generous support, insight, and positive feedback. Your enthusiasm towards customer service is inspirational. Your insightful blog and book are a gift to the dental community worldwide. Your devotion to customer service and kindness to your dental colleagues are most admirable. It is a pleasure to know you.

Thank you to customer service expert Shep Hyken. Your books, talks, videos, blog, and social media posts keep our fires for customer service burning. Thank you for sharing your insight and wealth of customer service knowledge with us.

A sincere thank you to bestselling author Dave Kerpen of Likeable Social Media. It was a thrill for me to meet with you in person in New York City, to visit the famous salad bar with the little orange bowl, and to share my excitement with you for this new book. You are an inspiration to all business owners and authors.

Thank you to Joan Garbo, a woman of positive enthusiasm, insight, and encouragement. You have delighted so many of us in dentistry through your coaching, speaking, and friendship. You are bright light and inspiration to us all. Thank you from the bottom of my heart for your contribution and encouragement with this book.

A heartfelt thank you to Rock Star orthodontist, Dr. Jay Bowman. Your enthusiasm for patient relations and office creativity is infectious and exemplary for us all. I admire you so much for the excellence you present in every aspect of the orthodontic profession. I am so happy to call you my friend.

A special thank you to Tal Shnall for his passion for customer service and customer service coaching. Your Facebook page is a valuable resource for anyone interested in customer service or working in a service industry. Your expertise from the field of hotel hospitality was valuable in the creation of this book.

Thank you to Dr. Bill Williams, author of *The Million Dollar Practice*. Your book is one of the best ever written for dentistry. I am delighted to have you part of this dental customer service project.

Thank you to Andre Shirdan of the C. R. E. W. (Philosophy, People, Process, Profitability) for his enthusiasm for this project and dedication to dental practice management and coaching. Your cheers for teamwork and self-motivation are a battle cry for customer service excellence.

Thank you to my sister, Dr. Diane Gorczyca Patrick for her customer service insight and examples from the field of medicine. Your tireless edits are very much appreciated. I am thankful and proud to call you my sister.

Thank you to my publisher, Stephanie Chandler of Authority Publishing, and Susan Cain, project manager, for their assistance and advice in the writing of my third book. It is always a pleasure to work with you.

Thank you to my loving husband for his contribution of brilliant and dedicated editorial work, which has helped to make this project completed and a success. All my love to my husband Richard, and my son Richard, who share my writing adventures with me every step of the way with curiosity, wonder, patience, forbearance, and love.

Thank you to all of you who have purchased this book and read it to the end. Thank you to all of my readers for their five-star reviews on Amazon. I am forever *At Your Service*. It is a pleasure to serve you. Thank you from the bottom of my heart.

-Ann Marie Gorczyca, DMD, MPH, MS
The Sea Ranch, California

ABOUT THE AUTHOR

The customer is our highest priority.
-Dr. Ann Marie Gorczyca

Dr. Ann Marie Gorczyca is a Clinical Adjunct Professor of Orthodontics at the Arthur A. Dugoni School of Dentistry, University of the Pacific, where she teaches practice management. Customer service is the fourth lecture of a six-part series that also includes marketing, teamwork, treatment coordination, customer service, systems management, and human resource management.

Dr. Gorczyca is a Diplomate of the American Board of Orthodontics, a member of the Angle Society of Orthodontists, and a graduate of Advanced Education in Orthodontics (Roth Course). She is a member of the Seattle Study Club, the American Association of Orthodontists (AAO), the Pacific Coast Society of Orthodontists (PCSO), the California Association of Orthodontists (CAO), the American Dental Association (ADA), the California Dental Association (CDA), and the Contra Costa Dental Society. She was an orthodontic associate of Dr. T. M. Graber in Evanston, Illinois. She has worked in a multispecialty group practice in Fairfield, California, and she has been a practicing orthodontist in Antioch, California, for twenty-seven years.

Dr. Gorczyca was graduated from Wellesley College, the Harvard School of Dental Medicine, the Harvard School of Public Health, and Northwestern University. She has studied at the Harvard School of Public Health's Department of Health Management and Policy, and she holds a Master's Degree in Public Health. She is active in her local dental com-

ABOUT THE AUTHOR

munity Seattle Study Club. She has served on the AAO Council of Communications and ADA National Boards Part II Test Construction Committee. She is past Treasurer of the Northern California Edward H. Angle Society of orthodontists and has served as a Board Member for the Pacific Coast Society of Orthodontists.

Dr. Gorczyca is the author of the books *It All Starts with Marketing—201 Marketing Tips for Growing a Dental Practice*, and *Beyond the Morning Huddle—HR Management for a Successful Dental Office*. She was a speaker at the 2011, 2012, 2014, 2015, 2016, and 2017 AAO Annual Sessions. She lives in Walnut Creek and The Sea Ranch, California, with her husband and son. This is her third book.

BIBLIOGRAPHY

Alcorn, Stacey. *The 5 Best Business Mantras From 'Mr. Wonderful'* https://www.entrepreneur.com/article/248321. July 27, 2015

Bacal, Rober. *Perfect Phrases for Customer Service*. New York, New York. McGraw Hill Education, 2011.

Bachelder, Cheryl. *Dare to Serve*. Oakland, California. Berrett-Koehler Publishers, Inc., 2015.

Baer, Jay. *Hug Your Haters*. New York, New York. Portfolio Penguin, 2016

Barnes, Roy, Kelleher, Bob. *Customer Experience for Dummies*. Hoboken, New Jersey. John Wiley & Sons, 2015.

Blanchard, Ken. *Legendary Service*. New York, New York. McGraw-Hill Education, 2014

Bliss, Jeanne. *Chief Customer Officer*. Hoboken, New Jersey. John Wiley & Sons. 2015.

Bliss, Jeanne. *I Love You More Than My Dog*. New York, New York, Penguin Group, 2009.

Cabane, Olivia Fox. *The Charisma Myth*. New York, New York. Portfolio/Penguin, 2013.

Cardone, Grant. *The 10X Rule*. Hoboken, New Jersey. John Wiley & Sons, Inc., 2011.

Cooper, Frank. *The Customer Signs Your Paycheck*. New York, New York. McGraw-Hill, 2010.

Cutting, Donna. *501 Ways to Roll Out the Red Carpet for your Customer*. Wayne, New Jersey. The Career Press, Inc., 2016.

DiJulius, John R., *The Customer Service Revolution*. Austin, Texas. Greenleaf Book Group Press, 2015.

Drahata, A., Costall, A., and Reddy, V. *The Vocal Communication of Different Kinds of Smiles*. Speech Communication 50, 4 (2008): 278.

Farran, Howard. *Uncomplicate Business*. Austin, Texas. Greenleaf Book Group Press, 2015.

Gitomer, Jeffrey. *Little Gold Book of YES! Attitude*. Upper Saddle River, New Jersey. FT Press, 2007.

Gladwell, Malcolm. *Outliers*. New York, New York. Back Bay Books/Little, Brown and Company, 2011.

Godin, Seth. *Poke the Box*. Do You Zoom, Inc. United States of America, 2011.

Goleman, Daniel, et al. *On Emotional Intelligence*. Boston, Massachusetts. Harvard Business School Publishing Corporation, 2015.

Gross, T. Scott. *Positively Outrageous Service*. New York, New York. Warner Books, 1991.

Harvey, Eric. *180 Ways to Walk the Customer Service Talk*. Flower Mound, Texas. Performance Publishing, 2016.

HBR Reprint F1701A, *The Power of Positive Surveying*. Harvard Business Review, January-February, 22-24, 2017.

Heffernan, Margaret. *Beyond Measure*. New York, Simon & Schuster, 2015.

Hsieh, Tony. *Delivering Happiness*. New York, New York. Hachette Book Group, 2010.

http://www.jyi.org/issue/trust-in-the-dentist-patient-relationship-a-review/ June, 2005

http://www.livescience.com/48407-americans-trust-docotors-falling.html September 12, 2016.

http://www.success.com/article/rohn/rohn-7-personality-traits-of-a-great-leaderAugust15, 2016.

http://soulsentences.wordpress.com/2012/07/16/your-name-the-most-beautiful-sound-you-can-hear-in-a-lifetime/ July 16, 2012.

http://sroutsocial.com/insights/index/q2-2016. Shunning Your Customers on Social? Sprout Social, May 15, 2016.

http://www.success.com/article/10-quick-tips-to-be-a-better-boss? March 19, 2015

http://thethrivingsmallbusiness.com/customer-wait-times-6-strategies-to-manage-wiating-customers/ September 26, 2011.

Hyken, Shep. *Amaze Every Customer Every Time*. Austin, Texas. Greenleaf Book Group Press, 2013

Hyken, Shep. *The Amazement Revolution*. Austin, Texas. Greenleaf Book Group Press, 2011.

Hyken, Shep. *The Cult of the Customer*. Hoboken, New Jersey. John Wiley & Sons, Inc. 2009.

Kaufman, Ron. *Uplifting Service*. www.evolvepublishing.com. Evolve Publishing, Inc., 2012.

Kerpen, Dave. *Likeable Business*. New York. McGraw Hill, 2013.

Kerpen, Dave. *Likeable Social Media*. New York, New York. The McGraw-Hill Companies, 2011.

Loeffler, Bruce, and Church, Brian T. *The Experience-The 5 Principles of Disney Service and Relationship Excellence*. Hoboken, New Jersey. Wiley, 2015.

Martins, Flavio. *Is Safety a Part of Customer Service?* http://www.business2community.com/customer-experience/safety-part-customer-service-0722603.

Martins, Flavio. *Win the Customer*. New York, New York. American Management Association, 2016.

Marwizi, Archibalk. *Five-Star Customer Service*. Harare, Zimbabwe. Gudbank Investments, 2015

Michelli, Joseph A., *The New Gold Standard*. New York, New York. McGraw-Hill, 2008.

Mitchell, Jack. *Hug Your Customers*. New York, New York. Hachette Books, 2015.

Moffet, Dr. David. *How to Build the Dental Practice of Your Dreams*. Charleston, South Carolina. Advantage, 2015.

Sauro, Jeff. *Customer Analytics for Dummies*. Hoboken, New Jersey. John Wiley & Sons, 2015.

Shankman, Peter. *Zombie Loyalists*. New York, New York. Palgrave Macmillan Trade, 2015

Thaler, Linda Kaplan, and Koval, Robin. *The Power of Nice*. The Doubleday Broadway Publishing Group, a division of Random House, Inc., New York. 2006.

Toporek, Adam. *Be Your Customer's Hero*. New York, New York. American Management Association, 2015.

Wasswerman, Todd. *11 Things You Didn't Know About Yelp*, http://mashable.com/2012/09/03/10-yelp-facts/#_vj.nrixbSk7.

Williamson, Jim. *Service: Brief Lessons and Inspiring Stories*. Hong Kong. Compendium Publishing, 2003.

INDEX

Abrams, Elliot, 33
Ackerman, Diane, 159
action, 50–51
active listening, 47–49
Adair, Paul, 129
Adams, Douglas, 26
Adams, John Quincy, 19
alignment
   complaints and, 67
   front desk and, 63–64
   money and, 64
   office manager and, 64–66
   strengths and, 68–69
   team players and, 63
   teamwork, customer experience and, 61
Allstate, 13
Anderson, Gillian, 139
Anderson, Mac, 151, 156
annual customer service award, 79
apology, 74
appearance
   appearance killers, 129
   camera ready, 130
   patient perception, 128
   posture, body language, 127–128
   professional look, 128
   uniforms, uniform maintenance, 127, 129–130
Apple, 13
appreciation gifts, 180–181
Aristotle, 31, 83
Ash, Mary Kay, 45
ask, 171, 174

assistance
- appreciation, 169
- five characteristics, 166–169
- friendly, 166–167
- polite phrases, service language, 165–166
- positive, 167–168
- precise, 168–169
- supportive, 167
- timely, 168

attention, consistency, 43

attitude
- eight ways to build positive work environment, 100–101
- eliminating negatives, 102–103
- four ways to always say YES, 101–102
- is everything, 105–106
- NO attitude, 103–104
- three ways to improve, 104–105
- YES attitude, 99–102

Avis, 13
award, 79
award tokens, 94

bad news, 118
Bain & Company, 165
Bandy, Jayne, 36, 44
Barnes, Roy, 108
before and after photos, 96
Beyond the Morning Huddle: HR Management for a Successful Dental Office (Gorczyca), 41, 109, 127
Bezos, Jeff, 45, 137, 207
Bliss, Jeanne, 187
Bone, Sterling, 72
boss, 189
boss-employee relationship, 111
Boswell, Nelson, 183
Bowman, Jay, 179–180
brand, branding, 111
- culture, 1–2
- engagement, 111

Branson, Richard, 28, 102

breakdown, 145
building exterior, wayfinding, 154–155

calendar template, 211, 212
call, 173–174
camera ready appearance, 130
can do, 41–42
care calls, 96–97
Carnegie, Dale, 158
Carrier Debora, 129
Chafee, Lincoln, 23
cheerleaders, 181–182
chief customer officer (CCO), 135
children's play area, 195
Chung, Alexa, 56
cleanliness, 153–154, 157
climate, temperature, patient perception, 137–138
collecting, 141
Collins, Jim, 197
communication
    active listening, 47–49
    alignment, 58–59
    attention, consistency and, 43
    concierge, 45
    emotional control, 50
    eye contact, 48–49
    four rules, 47–50
    greeting the patient, 51–52
    HIPAA, 57
    initial phone call, 44–45
    interruption, 48
    messaging system, 44–45
    missed appointment, 51
    negative communication, 56–57
    paraphrasing customer communication, 49
    photographic, 57
    politeness and, 49–50
    printed materials, 58
    small talk, 52
    taking action, 50–51

    ten most powerful customer service phrases, 52–56
    three steps of customer service, 46–47
    written, 58
compiling, 141–142
complaints, 67, 72
    four types of complainers, 74–75
    seven steps to handling, 73–74
completion celebration, Debond Day, 95
compliments, 71
concierge, front desk, 33, 37, 45, 63–64, 155–156
conduct, 82
confidence, 150
contests, giveaways, 95
Cooper, Frank, 69, 74, 79
core values, 2, 12
correcting, 142
Covey, Stephen, 10, 27, 58, 163
creating happiness, 183
creativity
    appreciation gifts, 180–181
    creating happiness, 183
    decorations, 186
    ephemera, gifts, 184–185
    innovation, team and, 183–184
    Jay Bowman, 179–180
    office cheerleaders, 181–182
    office themes, 185
    Shelby Smith, 180
    Smile Day, 181–182
cross-contamination, 194
cross-training, 40
culture
    brand and, 1–2
    core values and, 2
    customer service goals and, 2
    developing, 1
    leadership, training and, 2
    team members and, 2–3
Curtin, Steve, 99
customer as boss, 189–190
customer feedback collection, 141

customer journey map, 149
Customer Relations Management (CRM), 111–113
customer service, 87. *See also* five-star customer service
    apology, three parts, 74
    calendar template, 211, 212
    four Cs, 140–142
    goals, 2
    as the new marketing, 207
    phrases, 52–56, 69–70
    rating, 191
    strongest leader and, 17–18
    three steps, 46–47
The Customer Signs Your Paycheck (Cooper), 69, 74

da Vinci, Leonardo, 151
Danzie, Jay, 119
David, Jim, 22
Davidson & Licht, 204
de Valera, Eamon, 145
Debond Day, 95
decorations, 186
dental office mantra, 61–63
Dental Phone Excellence, 36
dental spa, 97, 161–162
Dental Support Specialties, 40
Disney, Roy, 12
Disneyland, 37, 39, 132, 159, 160
doctor time, 39
Drahota smile study, 120
Drucker, Peter, 13, 190
Dupree, Ken, 97
Dyer, Wayne, 52

Eastman, Max, 32
Edison, Thomas A., 124
education, cross-training, staffing, 2, 11, 40–41, 133–134
effective customer service phrases, 69–70
eight ways to build positive work environment, 100–101
Einstein, Albert, 22, 193, 207

Einstein Medical Center, 198
Eisner, Michael, 153
emotional control, 50
empowerment
  breakdowns and, 145
  building, 149–150
  communicating and, 142–143
  compiling and, 141–142
  correcting, management systems and, 142
  customer feedback collection, 141
  customer journey map and, 149
  four Cs of customer service, 140–150
  inefficiencies and, 145–146
  mistakes and, 143–144
  The ONE Thing, 147–148
  rework, 144–145
  team competency, 139–140
  the Ts, 147–148
  variations and, 146–147
engagement
  assessment of, 107
  boss-employee relationship, 111
  branding, 111
  Customer Relations Management (CRM), 111–113
  by doctor, 108
  five ways to build team engagement, 110–111
  laughter, fun and, 111
  office goals and, 110
  social media, 112–114
  social media, customer engagement, 114–115
  social media, customer reviews, 116–118
  team environment, EX-CX, 109–110
  three steps of engagement, 108–109
  2013 Gallup Poll, State of the American Workplace, 107
  Yelp, 115–117
environment, 195
ephemera, gifts, 184–185
Epictetus, 47
escorting, 192–193
excellence
  achieving, 85

culture of, 84–85
helpfulness and, 81–82
office reward system and, 83
team excellence, 83–84
thirteen action items for, 83
eye contact, 48–49
eyes, 192

fan, 177
Farran, Howard, 108
feel, 164
fifteen patient-friendly experiences, 91–98
final treatment letter, 175
first impression for last impression, 204
The Five Levels of Leadership (Maxwell), 5
five senses, 151–163
five ways to build team engagement, 110–111
five-star customer service
    adding value to patient experience, 203
    customer service as the new marketing, 207
    first impression for last impression, 204
    five-star reviews, 207
    going the extra mile, 201–202
    greeting patients with a smile, 203
    legendary customer service, 205
    platinum rule, 205
    service inspired life, 207–208
    small acts of kindness, 202
    staying true to five-star values, 206
    three customer service essentials, 202–203
    values, 206
five-star reviews, 207
flavored gloves, 93
floors, carpeting, sidewalks, 193
Follett, Mary Parker, 73
formal survey, 172–173
four Cs of customer service, 140–150
four customer service measurements, 190–191
four rules of communication, 47–50
four tips for handling customer stress, 188–198

four types of complainers, 74–75
four ways to always say YES, 101–102
friendliness
    award, 94
    before and after photos, 96
    care calls and, 96–97
    completion celebration, Debond Day, 95
    contests, giveaways and, 95
    customer needs and, 89
    dental spa experience, 97
    fifteen patient-friendly experiences, 91–98
    flavored gloves, 93
    friends of business list, 91–92
    hygienic kits, goody bags, 93
    likeable team and, 89
    office T-shirts, 94
    patient appreciation day, 94–95
    patient experience and, 90
    special cards and, 96
    surprises, gifts, 92–93
    tooth whitening gifts, 94
    welcome questionnaire, 91
friendly, 90, 166
friends of business list, 91–92
Fritz, Jerry, 84
front desk, 45, 63–64
fulfillment
    asking, patient responses, 171–172
    final treatment letter, 175
    formal survey, 172–173
    non-start patients, calls, 173–174
    patient happiness assessment, 175–176
    postcard survey, 172
    Press-Ganey survey, 173
    redo dentists, 177
    satisfaction guarantee, 174–175
    six forms of customer feedback, 171–174
    team member feedback, 175
    ten-year retainer checks, 175
    VIP feedback, 173
fun activities, 90, 166

fun work, patient climate, 198–199

Galante, Donna, 191
Garvey, Marcus, 152
Gates, Bill, 171
Gibbon, Edward, 131
Gitomer, Jeffrey, 91
Gladwell, Malcolm, 208
Godin, Seth, 81, 205
Goldsmith, Marshall, 32
Gorczyca, Ann Marie, 41, 109, 127, 141, 217
Gorczyca Orthodontics, 13, 14
Greenleaf, Robert K., 24
greeting the patient, 51–52, 203

Hansel Auto Group, 15
happiness, 119, 175, 183
Harvard Business School, 116
Harvey, Eric, 10, 52
health safety, 193–194
Heffernan, Margaret, 1, 147
HIPAA, 57
Holloway, Darnell, 115–116
Holmes, Anissa, 161
Holtz, Lou, 96
How to Build the Dental Practice of Your Dreams in Less Than 60 Days Without Killing Yourself (Moffet), 21
Hsieh, Tony, 16, 17, 82, 166
Hurley, Janice, 130
hygienic kits, goody bags, 93
Hyken, Shep, 12, 17, 134, 188, 205

I'M NOT OK-YOU'RE NOT OK, anti-social narcissistic relationship, 76–77
I'M NOT OK-YOU'RE OK, juvenile relationship, 75
I'M OK-YOU'RE NOT OK, cynical relationship, 76
I'M OK-YOU'RE OK, healthy relationship, 75
impossible patients, 77
impression

    acting the part, 132–133
    building patient experience, cross-training, 133–134
    chief customer officer (CCO), 135
    lasting impressions, 135
    scripting, 133
    surprises for customers, 134
    wow! moment, 131–132
inefficiencies, 145–146
initial phone call, 33–34, 44–45
initial welcome, 32–33
innovation, team, 183–184
inspiration, 207
integrity, 26
interruption, 48
Invisalign, 145
It All Starts with Marketing—201 Marketing Tips for a Successful Dental Practice (Gorczyca), 141

J. C. Penny, 184
Jamaica Cosmetic Dental Services, 161
Jobs, Steve, 11
joy, 123–124

Kaiser-Permanente, 13
Kaufman, Ron, 149
Kawasaki, Guy, 122
Kelleher, Bob, 108
Keller, Gary, 147
Kerpen, Dave, 24, 180
kindness, 203
Kissinger, Henry, 37
know patients, 68
Kotter, John, 10

late, 38
laughter, fun, 111
Le Boeuf, Michael, 174
leadership

    boldness and, 19
    challenge of, 19–20
    ethics and, 8
    humility, pride and, 19
    influence, 7
    kindness and, 19–20
    self-control and, 20
    training, 2
    transformational, 5–6, 20
    trust and, 20
    truth and, 5
leadership, five Rs
    recruitment, 11–12
    relationships, 8–11
    respect, 7–8
    results, 10–11
    right, 6–7
lease, 196–197
least happy customers, three questions to ask, 72
Leeds, Dorothy, 209
legendary customer service, 205
Leonard, Stew, 74
Likeable Business (Kerpen), 24
Likeable Leadership (Kerpen), 180
Lombardi, Vince, 28
lost customers, 71
Lowndes, Leil, 120
Luca, Michael, 116
lunch food, 160

Maltoni, Valeria, 90
management systems, 71
management systems, correcting, 142
mantras, external, 61–62
mantras, internal, 61–62
mantras, problem solving, 63
marketing, 207
Martins, Flavio, ix–xii
Maslow, Abraham, 193
Maxwell, John, 5, 6, 8, 20, 103

McKain, Scott, 132
measurements, 190–191
medical safety, 194–195
mediocre customer service phrases, 70
messaging system, 44–45
Meyer, Joyce, 38
Michelli, Joseph, 83
The Millimeter Approach (Galante), 191
mindfulness, 124
missed appointment, 51
mission statement, 12–14
mistakes, 143–144
Moffet, David, 21, 36
money, 64
Morley, Christopher, 153
Mother Teresa, 124, 209
MR. BIV, 142–149
My Fair Lady, 165
my pleasure, 176
My Social Practice, 125, 185

name, 46, 51, 158
Nasser, Kate, 116
negative communication, 56–57
negatives, 102–103
The New Gold Standard (Michelli), 83
NO attitude, 103–104
non-doctor days, 40
non-start patients, calls, 173–174
Novak, Robby, 135
Noyse, William, 213

office cheerleaders, 181–182
Office Cleanliness Coordinator (OCC), 153
office environment, unwanted visits, phone calls, 195
office goals, 110
office lease, 196–197
office manager and, 64–66
office property protection, 195–196

office reputation, 197–198
office reward system, 83
office schedule, 163–164
office temperature, 162
office themes, 185
office T-shirts, 94
O'Leary, Kevin, 63
Olivieri, Mark, 55
180 Ways to Walk the Customer Service Talk (Harvey), 10, 52
Outliers (Gladwell), 208
ownership
   cross-training, staffing, 40–41
   doctor time, 39
   front desk concierge, patient interaction and, 33
   gratitude, thank you and, 40
   non-doctor days, 40
   ownership questions, 32
   patient initial phone call and, 33–34
   patient initial welcome and, 32–33
   phone etiquette, 35, 40
   phone service, after school, 35
   phone service, after-hours calls, pagers, 36
   phone service, morning and lunchtime, 35
   phone service, voicemail, 36
   problem solving and, 31–32
   reception area, 37
   responsibility and, 31
   running late, 38–39
   scheduling, 36–37
ownership questions, 32

pagers, 36
Panucci, Donna, 181
Panwar, Nishan, 67
Papasan, Jay, 147
paraphrasing customer communication, 49
Parature, 90
Parenta, Frank, 102
Pasternak, Boris, 92
patient appreciation day, 94–95

Patient Bill of Rights, 27
patient escorting, 193
patient experience, 91–98, 133
patient eye protection, 192
patient happiness assessment, 175–176
patient initial phone call, 33–34
patient initial welcome, 32–33
Peabody, Francis, 87
perseverance, 187–188
personal responsibility, 31
Peters, Tom, 187
phone service
    after school, 35
    after-hours calls, pagers, 36
    calls answered percentage, 190
    etiquette, 35, 40, 121
    morning, lunchtime, 35
    phone etiquette, 121–122
    voicemail, 36
photographic communication, 57
Pickett, Tom, 171
platinum rule, 205
Plomer, William, 179
Poke the Box (Godin), 81
politeness, 49–50
poor customer service phrases, 70
Porter, Donald, 143
Porter, Michael, 124
positive, 167
Post, Emily, 34
postcard survey, 172
posture, body language, 127–128
precise, 168
preparedness
    building exterior, wayfinding, 154–155
    cleanliness, 153–154
    dental spa, 161–162
    five senses and, 151–163
    lunch food, 160
    Office Cleanliness Coordinator (OCC), 153
    office schedule and, 163–164

office temperature, 162
patient feeling right, 164
reception area, 155–156
restrooms, 156–157
sense of sight and, 152–153
sense of smell and, 159–160
sense of sound and, 158
sense of taste and, 162–163
sense of touch and, 161
sterilization, cleanliness, 157
treatment areas, 156
preservation, Management of Systems
children's play area, 195
cross-contamination, 194
customer as boss, 189–190
customer service rating, 191
floors, carpeting, sidewalks, 193
four customers service measurements, 190–191
four tips for handling customer stress, 188–198
fun work, patient climate, 198–199
health safety, 193–194
medical safety, 194–195
office environment, unwanted visits, phone calls, 195
office lease, 196–197
office property protection, 195–196
office reputation, 197–198
patient escorting, 193
patient eye protection, 192
perseverance, 187–188
phone calls answered percentage, 190
safety, 191–192
same day starts, 190
will call starts, 191
Press-Ganey survey, 28, 173
Prichard, Skip, 6
printed materials, 58
professional look, 128
property, 195–196

Radcliffe, Paula, 49

rating, 191
reception area, 155
redo dentists, 177
relationships, 18
Rell, Jodi, 191
reputation, 197–198
restrooms, 156–157
results
    annual customer service award and, 79
    complainers, four types of, 74–75
    complaints, seven steps to handling, 73–74
    complaints and, 72
    compliments and, 71
    customer service apology, three parts, 74
    effective customer service phrases, 69–70
    I'M NOT OK-YOU'RE NOT OK, anti-social narcissistic relationship, 76–77
    I'M NOT OK-YOU'RE OK, juvenile relationship, 75
    I'M OK-YOU'RE NOT OK, cynical relationship, 76
    I'M OK-YOU'RE OK, healthy relationship, 75
    impossible patients and, 77
    least happy customers, three questions to ask, 72
    lost customers and, 71
    management systems and, 71
    mediocre customer service phrases, 70
    poor customer service phrases, 70
    service recovery and, 78
    surveys and, 71–72
    tracking, 79
reviews, 118
reward, 83
reworks, 144–145
Richards, Damon, 164
The Ritz-Carlton, 16, 54, 83, 141, 142 156
Rohn, Jim, 19
Rumsfeld, Donald, 140
running late, 38–39

safety, 191–192. *See also* preservation, Management of Systems
    health safety, 193–194
    medical safety, 194–195

same day starts, 190
Sand, George, 175
Sanders, Dan, 139
Sartre, Jean-Paul, 107
satisfaction guarantee, 174–175
scent, 159, 160
scheduling, 36–37, 163–164
Schultz, Howard, 162
Schulz, Horst, 115
scripting, 123
service inspired life, 207–208
service recovery, 78
Severson, Dana, 111
Shankman, Peter, 91
Shark Tank, 63
Siegel, Bernie, 161
sight, 152–153
Sinek, Simon, 16, 48, 181
six forms of customer feedback, 171–174
small acts of kindness, 202
small talk, 52
smell, 159–160
smile
   Drahota study, 120
   fun and, 124–125
   health benefits of, 120
   joy and, 124
   mindfulness and, 124
   My Social Practice patient campaigns, 125
   service, happiness with, 119–120
   Social Progress Index (Porter), 124
   telephone etiquette and, 121–122
Smile Day, 181–182
Smith, Shelby, 180
social media, 112–114
   customer engagement, 114–115
   customer reviews, 116–118
Social Progress Index (Porter), 124
sound, 158
special cards, 96
Sprout Social, 112, 113, 114

Star Wars, 179–180
Stengel, Casey, 61
sterilization, cleanliness, 157
Stoller, Goodall & Baker, 64
Sund, David, 99
supportive, 167
surprises, gifts, 92–93, 134
surveys, 28, 71–72, 172–173
Suttle, Marilyn, 71
Swartz Center for Compassionate Healthcare (SCCH), 99

tag line, 14
taste, 162–163
team, teamwork, 2–3, 16–17, 63, 109–110
    alignment, 63
    competency, 139–140
    creativity, innovation, 183–184
    culture, 2–3
    customer experience and, 61
    empowerment, competency, 139–140
    engagement, 109–110
    excellence, 83–84
    EX-CX, 110
    feedback, 175
    innovation, 183–184
    likeable team, friendliness, 89
    member feedback, 175
    team member trust, 28–29
TEDx, 22
telephone etiquette, 35, 40, 121
temperature, 162
ten most powerful customer service phrases, 52–56
ten-year retainer checks, 175
thank you, 39–40, 53
The ONE Thing (Keller, Papasan), 147–148
the Ts, 147–148
themes, 168
Thich Nhat Hahn, 120
thirteen action items for excellence, 83
three customer service essentials, 202–203

three elements of trust, 22–23
three steps of customer service, 46–47
three steps of engagement, 108–109
three ways to improve attitude, 104–105
TIME, 89
timely, 168
tooth whitening gifts, 94
touch, 161
tracking, 79
treatment areas, 156
Triggers (Goldsmith), 32
trust
    ability and, 23–24
    benevolence and, 24–25
    building, 21, 23, 27–28
    doctor trust, 27–28
    employees and, 26
    integrity and, 26
    micromanagement and, 29
    patient interaction and, 21–22, 24–25
    perception of, 22
    personalized assistance philosophy and, 22
    shared-decision making and, 28
    team member trust, 28–29
    three elements of, 22–23
Tseng, Yani, 121
212 Degree Service (Anderson), 156
2013 Gallup Poll, State of the American Workplace, 107

Ultimate Patient Experience, 36
Uncomplicated Business (Farran), 108
uniforms, uniform maintenance, 127, 129–130
Ursino, Mark, 43, 78

Vaill, George, 196–197
value, 203
variations, 147
VIP feedback, 173
Virgin America Airlines, 28

vision, 14–15
Voltaire, 94

Walt Disney World, 10, 16
Walton, Sam, 40, 71, 189
wayfinding, 154
Welcome, 169
welcome questionnaire, 91
why?, 16
will call starts, 191
Williams, Heather, 206
Williams, Jim, 133
Williamson, Jim, 196
Wooden, John, 7
Wow!, 131
written communication, 58

Yelp, 115–117
YES
   attitude, 99–102
   phrase, 52–53
   say, 101–102

Zabriskie, Kate, 118
Zappos, 13, 17, 81–82
Ziglar, Zig, 40
Zombie Loyalists (Shankman), 91